ILLINOIS
HAUNTED
ROUTE 66

JANICE TREMEEAR

Haunted
America

Published by Haunted America
A Division of The History Press
Charleston, SC 29403
www.historypress.net

Unless otherwise noted, all images are in the public domain.

First published 2013

Manufactured in the United States

ISBN 978.1.62619.252.2

Library of Congress CIP data applied for.

CONTENTS

Acknowledgements   5
Introduction   7

1. Illinois and Route 66: From the Beginning   9
2. Chicago   18
3. Joliet   60
4. Watseka   70
5. Bloomington   81
6. Springfield   86
7. New Salem   97
8. Cahokia   101

Bibliography   109
About the Author   112

Acknowledgements

To Dean, my life partner: I could not function as well as an author and speaker without your continued support and belief in me. My children, Jennifer Burgmeyer, Charlene Wells and Nathaniel Wells, are always rooting Mom on and expecting the best from me. My grandkids, Geoffrey Burgmeyer, Madison Burgmeyer, Tonia Burgmeyer, Erica Varga and Sheridan Varga, think "Grandma Jees is cool" and say, "Well, that's just you, Grandma." Thanks to Mardee Robins, Charlene's school classmate, who braved the trip as a teen with Charlene into Satan's Tunnel at Hawk's Point, Missouri, where a shadow man followed them home and lurked outside our front door, launching me into my full-blown paranormal journey. Thanks to Dave and Kim Dewitt for firsthand accounts. Thanks to Sara Preston for her support. Special thanks to Philip Booth of Spooked TV for his movie *The Possessed* and the sharing of experiences the Booths had during filming.

INTRODUCTION

G hosts, UFOs and odd creatures linger just outside our line of sight, notoriously refusing to leave behind written trails and contrary to having their photos taken. They are insidious and addictive, luring us in with sounds, glimpses of movement, a fragrance, unexplained dreams or memories, generational experiences or our own personal encounters—which may often alienate us from our own families should we admit to them in public. The questions of life beyond our planet or after death beckon and tease, waiting for us to pay full attention, to catch them at their game of hide-and-seek, driving us forward to be bold in discovering what's "out there." They may come nose to nose with us, hoping to break through our veil of ignorance for all things supernatural, hoping we'll hear and see that world lurking outside our comfort zone, beyond the realm of what we deem sane, adult reasoning. We in the flesh strive to maintain our "feet upon the ground" as we quest to achieve both monetary and social status in false belief that this makes us whole as human beings. But in the core of our primitive mind is the "what if," the "dare we brave the unknown and unfamiliar," and that's what drives me to search out the paranormal.

CHAPTER 1

ILLINOIS AND ROUTE 66
FROM THE BEGINNING

G et Your Kicks on Route 66," the famous song written by Bobby Troup, brings to mind the freewheeling, fun attitude of vacationing families seeking adventure and new sights as they traveled along the "Middle Road" or the more oft-turned phrase, "Mother Road of North America," as coined by John Steinbeck. The call for adventure lured with promises of spicy sights and racy tales of roadside dives.

Called the "most magical road in all the world" with its roadside giants, campsites, mini museums, mom-and-pop businesses, motor courts and eateries topped with miles upon miles of glowing neon, Route 66 was a lighted pathway enticing the weary, delighting the wide-eyed seekers of the wonder of the open road. Cozy Dog Drive-in, the historic eatery in Springfield, Illinois, is the home to the original hot dog on a stick. Established in 1949, the drive-in served as one of the enticing oddities people loved.

Some believe Route 66 embodies a part of the "dragon lines," a very powerful energy grid located at specific longitude and latitude lines, known as ley lines, which create sacred geometric grid patterns on the globe where many ancient sites and spirit roads exist, such as the Mayan and the Egyptian pyramids. In between Chicago and Los Angeles runs the shattered spine of America, the broken ley line of Route 66, with the main break appearing in Kansas.

A growing population during the 1920s and a growing number of automobiles forced highway officials to admit to the impracticality of disjointed trails. Legislation for public highways first appeared in 1916.

Congress enacted an even more comprehensive version of the act in 1925 and executed its plan for national highway construction. Cyrus Avery, a Tulsa, Oklahoma resident, teamed with highway proponent John Woodruff of Springfield, Missouri, to lobby for the creation of a diagonal roadway running from Chicago to Los Angeles.

The American Association of State Highway and Transportation Officials (AASHTO) named the road Route 60 and then changed it to Route 62. Avery "strenuously objected" to the switch, sending an impassioned letter to AASHTO executive secretary William Markham that read, "You are making a joke of the interstate highway." On April 30, 1926, the route became Route 66. Avery gained fame as the "Father of Route 66," the birthplace of which was located in Springfield, Missouri.

Illinois begins the great roadside culture with the 2,448-mile-long asphalt python starting in the downtown Chicago loop at the "slabbed" Pontiac Trail, SBI 4. Like the tip of the Yellow Brick Road in *The Wizard of Oz*, the section of Route 66 constructed during 1926 to 1930 is the most scenic part in Illinois, slanting through a densely populated, developed state with a fairly level alignment thanks to the scraping of Ice Age glaciers—unlike the twists, switchbacks, cuts and roller-coaster terrain it takes in Missouri, west of St. Louis. As early as the mid-1920s, the Prairie State boasted that its segment of the Old Road was mud-free and slab all the way.

Postcard image of the Muffler Man.

"Muffler Men" were gentle giants bordering the road in front of tourist shops, service stations or restaurants. Once common in the heyday of Route 66, only a few of them survive. The most iconic one, "Tall Paul," holding a giant hotdog, is located in Atlanta, Illinois. It was moved (it originally stood in Cicero, Illinois) and beautifully restored by the Route 66 Association. Route 66 soon became the road of choice for Capone and other Chicago gangsters in the pursuit of wealth. During Prohibition, bootleg whiskey, speakeasies and roadhouses were at every turn. Tales spawned of rumrunners, gangsters and ladies of the evening lent a mythic, romantic image to the highway, giving it the wild quality some people sought to alleviate the boredom of daily life. They dared to take flight from the humdrum as they sought the riches of California on an exhilarating quest where a discovery of the unknown, unusual and bizarre was synonymous with fun and adventure. The fairy-tale charm of Route 66 was its idiosyncratic personality, spreading forth like a giant carnival midway. This corridor of neon signs and gaudy roadside attractions was widely embraced by the eager traveling public.

The status of Route 66 in American culture cannot be replaced by the soulless super-highway systems of today, yet it was extremely dangerous as "Bloody 66" twisted through congested cities, crossed busy railroads on grade and was riddled with blind corners or hazardous cross traffic. Most accidents happened at intersections with county roads or railroad crossings. A bad stretch north of Pontiac held the nickname Dead Man's Alley.

The Mother Road has been glorified in countless classic books, movies and even a TV series. The song "Route 66" has been covered over two hundred times by artists including Rosemary Clooney, the Andrew Sisters, Michael Martin Murphey, the Rolling Stones, Nat King Cole and the Cramps. Its legendary status in pop culture is justified: America's soul is laid out in a line for everyone to see. Illinois was the first state to hard surface the highway and the first to replace it with interstate. It was where Route 66 began and, finally, where it was officially ended. Nothing can completely dull the allure of the "Main Street of America." Traveling this road was and is an extraordinary experience, a vital part of our American culture, the bloodline of the nation.

Indian tribes once roamed plains of prairie grass and wild onion bog, and the mounds of Illinois are objects of curiosity, controversy and mystery, as they were in Missouri. Even the first settlers yielded theories of the "mound-builders"—people who migrated from Asia or Mexico—and linked the structures to "faeries" or speculated that they were used as burial sites. Among the most intriguing of these sites are the effigy mounds that represent various animals. The Bureau of American Ethnology conducted a survey of the mounds in the eastern United States late in the twentieth century, resulting in a scientific view of the anomalies that described them as "raised both towns and places of worship on these artificial eminences. The human remains found in the mounds that have been excavated to date, are all of the American Indian type, and represent only the recent period

Route 66 Red Brick Road in an Illinois postcard.

of geologic time." Some are prehistoric, while others are proven by their contents as post-Columbian. Ancestors of the Winnebago and Sioux stock seem to be the closest in origin.

Add the haunted roads and wooded areas of Illinois or the ghosts in private homes as the Mother Road winds down to cross the Mississippi River in Missouri, and Route 66 is a hotbed of history and lore. From the first installment of the road in Illinois, it carried its history of ghosts and weird anomalies to the Show Me State and on into California, encompassing eight states and leaving behind a bloody past and hauntings still being researched today. For instance, take the now famous curse of the Billy Goat Tavern, located at 430 North Lower Michigan Avenue. William "Billy Goat" Sianis owned and operated the Billy Goat Tavern in Chicago, and he'd bring the tavern's mascot, his pet goat, to public events. In 1945, the Chicago Cubs played in the World Series against the Detroit Tigers. Sianis showed up with his pet goat and was denied admission. P.K. Wrigley, owner of the Cubs, stated that he didn't want the goat in the ballpark due to its smell. Sianis promptly placed a curse on the Chicago Cubs: they would never again win a pennant or World Series. It often appears the Cubs have broken the curse, but then they lose again. Efforts to dispel it have failed, and it remains in effect to this day (so the legend persists). The Billy Goat Tavern also experienced fame and glory though a *Saturday Night Live* skit featuring Dan Aykroyd and John Belushi.

Another odd tale is of Givins Castle, sitting snugly tucked in the south side neighborhood of Beverly. The castle was built by a man from Ireland for his wife, who never got to see the structure. She remained behind in Ireland and died before its completion, but she's now seen walking up the hill toward a home she never viewed.

Unidentified mysterious animals (UMAs) or cryptids dot the serene countryside; the famous flying cryptids are the thunderbirds, or piasa birds (pronounced PIE-a-saw and meaning "devourer of men"), in written accounts from Louis Joliet and Father Jacques Marquette. According to Joliet's diary, the piasa "was as large as a calf with horns like a deer, red eyes, a beard like a tiger's, a face like a man, the body covered with green, red and black scales and a tail so long it passed around the body, over the head and between the legs." A representation of the birdlike monster is painted high on the bluffs along the Mississippi River, where the city of Alton, Illinois, now stands. Thunderbirds have been reported throughout time and in many states and could create peals of thunder by the mere flap of their wings and shoot lighting from their eyes. The Cahokia Indians depicted this bird on the bluffs, perhaps as a warning from a tribe that conducted human sacrifice. This huge bird lives in legends of the Illini Indians, as well as the Sioux, Yaqui, Hoh, Quileute, Mayan, Yek and Corentyn. Often described with horned heads, scales, great beaks and claws large enough to pluck whales out of the sea, other legends say they were giant man-eating bats or large flying serpents. These creatures may have been condors or pterosaurs, judging by their descriptions. Another possibility is that the animal was a Quetzalcoatuls.

According to the autobiography of Blackhawk, a Sauk warrior, there was a cave containing the bones of the victims of this enormous bird. Large enough to carry off a man or deer, the bird preyed on the Native Americans. The painting above the river was called the Storm Bird or Thunder Bird. The piasa painting and description show the body of a dragon, mane of a lion, head of a bearded angry man with sharp teeth, deer antlers and a twelve-foot tail. Some pictures give the creature spiny wing scales, four birdlike legs and eagle talons. This beast developed a taste for humans after eating dead flesh and is a relative to the horned serpent.

One of the earliest official reports of a thunderbird attack was made in Tippah County, Missouri, just over the Mississippi River from Illinois in 1868. In 1948, sightings of thunderbirds came in a few times a month from Alton, Illinois. In 1977, in Lawndale in Logan County, Illinois, two giant birds attacked three young boys playing in their backyard. Near Delevan, Illinois, in 1977, a thunderbird snatched a sixty-pound hog from a pasture, flew to a telephone pole and proceeded to enjoy a leisurely meal, leaving the remains in the ditch.

Shawnee National Forest covers miles and miles of territory in the southern portion of the state and is referred to as the "Devil's Kitchen," a designation given to it by Native Americans and early settlers by reason of the strange sights, sounds, unexplained balls of light, apparitions, screams in the night and other various unsettling phenomena experienced here. The Native Americans considered these sites to be sacred, whereas the settlers believed them to be cursed.

The "Enfield Horror" remains one of the strangest creatures chronicled in cryptozoological lore. On April 25, 1973, in Enfield, Illinois, a young Greg Garrett was attacked by a four-and-a-half-foot-tall tripedal being covered in a grayish, slimy epidermis with stubby arms, short claws and reddish eyes. This creature stamped on the boy's feet with its own clawed, foot-like appendages, ripping his tennis shoes to shreds. Greg's encounter was the first on record, but the sighting bringing this creature to notoriety came when Garret's neighbor Henry McDaniel returned home at 9:30 p.m. to find two of his children, Henry Jr. and Lil, in a terrified stupor after their own face-to-face encounter with this unbelievable entity. The children claimed that while their parents were gone, a "thing" tried to break into the house through the door and a window-mounted air conditioner. Then they all heard a "scratching" sound at the front door, and upon opening the door to investigate, McDaniel faced the beast. Quickly slamming the door, he retrieved his .22-caliber revolver and then opened the door to confirm it wasn't a hallucination. He then opened fire on the creature. McDaniel claimed he hit it with all four rounds. The beast then reportedly "hissed like a wildcat" and fled across the McDaniel property and away into the darkness. McDaniel reported, "It had three legs on it, a short body, and two little short arms coming out of its breast area and two pink eyes as big as flashlights. It stood four and a half feet tall and was grayish-colored…it was trying to get into the house! When I fired that first shot, I know I hit it."

Illinois state troopers called to the scene did not see the creature itself but found scratches on the house's siding and a bizarre set of prints described as being dog-like, but with six toes and, importantly, a tripedal gait. On May 6, McDaniel was awoken by barking and howling from the neighborhood dogs. Grabbing his gun, he opened the front door to observe the creature moving through the rail trestles near his home. County Sherriff Roy Poshard Jr. threatened to incarcerate Mr. McDaniel for causing a panic, but McDaniel was exonerated when armed local groups patrolling the rail tracks sighted a similar being with a hairy pelt. It fled at high speed after they fired repeatedly at it. The final sighting was by a local radio news director, Rick Rainbow. He and three others (who requested anonymity) reported a five-foot-tall stooping creature near the Garret and McDaniel homes. Before the Enfield sighting, during the years of 1941 and 1942, Mt. Vernon, a sleepy little village less than forty miles away, experienced a similar spate of encounters.

In the 1970s, a rash of reports were filed regarding an upright walking bear, stories of giant black cats or a huge furred bipedal ape-like creature with glowing eyes terrorizing the state.

UFO sightings were often reported in the 1800s. On April 10, 1897, the *St. Louis Post-Dispatch* published a story reporting that one W.H. Hopkins encountered a grounded airship about twenty feet in length and eight feet in diameter near the outskirts of Springfield, Missouri. Among the most famous newspaper articles in the nineteenth century of airship sightings was written in the *St. Louis Democrat* on October

19, 1865. That same article appeared two weeks later in the *Cincinnati Commercial*, bringing more public awareness to UFOs. The account was of an old Montana fur trapper by the name of James Lumley who saw a UFO fly over him and crash into the forest, exploding like a rocket. The story was picked up by the *Missouri Democrat* and other newspapers, which contributed to national attention or awareness of alien spacecraft. During this era, there was a wave of activity. (A "UFO wave" is an unexplained increase in the number of UFO sightings over a certain period of time, usually building to a peak and then decreasing to normal. Waves generally cover a wide area. A "concentration" generally covers a much smaller area.)

On May 28, 1979, a Boy Scout leader took thirteen boys on a hike up Blueberry Hill in Franklin Park. At 3:45 p.m., after reaching the top of the hill, a high-pitched whine was heard coming from above. As the campers looked up, they saw a pulsating, metallic saucer twenty feet in diameter hovering fifty to sixty feet above the ground.

The famous "St. Clair Triangle," "UFO over Illinois," "Southern Illinois UFO" or "Highland, Illinois UFO" are nicknames for a UFO flap (an outbreak or flurries of UFO activity that can be quite intense and concentrated to localized areas) occurring about 4:00 a.m. on January 5, 2000, in St. Clair County, Illinois. Eight different police departments witnessed and pursued a huge triangular craft that "jumped" over twenty miles in mere seconds, traveling over the towns of Highland, Dupo, Lebanon, Summerfield, Millstadt and O'Fallon. Five on-duty Illinois police officers in separate locales and various other witnesses reported the massive, silent aircraft operating at an unusual range of movement from near-hover to incredible high speed at treetop altitudes. This incident was examined in the hour-long special *UFOs Over Illinois*, produced by Discovery Channel; an ABC special titled *Seeing Is Believing*, by Peter Jennings; and a Sci Fi Channel special entitled *Proof Positive*.

On July 12, 2000, in Downers Grove, Illinois, a building security guard witnessed a grouping of bright lights and "a huge object that was trying to land in the parking lot" at 8:00 p.m. He said, "It was as long as eight buses and almost as high." He described the object as dark silver/blue in color with a "goldish" stripe across it and a concave underside.

On February 2, 2002, just before midnight, students and residents of twin college towns Urbana-Champaign observed clusters of amber-hued lights flashing in a southwest to northeast line across the sky. A police officer watched the objects hover above Memorial Stadium, and he said there were all kinds of chatter about unidentified objects on his scanner that night. One witness noticed some buildings illuminated by spotlights originating from the objects.

In addition to the UFO sightings listed in this chapter, mythical Route 66 harbors hitchhiking ghosts, macabre horse-drawn hearses, encounters with the devil himself and whispered tales of black magic rituals in Chicago. The following chapters contain a smattering of the tales of the unknown that one can find linked to the state of Illinois, birthplace of President Abraham Lincoln.

CHAPTER 2

CHICAGO

It is hopeless for the occasional visitor to try to keep up with Chicago.
She outgrows his prophecies faster than he can make them.
—Mark Twain, 1883

Chicago ghosts wander the streets, but not all are the spirits of Depression-era gangsters. Indeed, the Windy City hosts wild haunts of ordinary men and women who continue to call Chicago "home" and cannot or will not leave the city. They are a lively, boisterous and rowdy congregation—for being dead.

Accounts from the 1600s indicate the Illinois Indians were the first people to claim a land they named "Chicaugou," meaning powerful, strong or great; this term was used by tribal chiefs signifying they were "great" chiefs. The name Chicago comes from a Miami Indian word for the wild leeks that grew on the bank of the short Chicago River. Over the centuries, the Miami, Sauk, Fox and Potawatomi tribes all lived in the area.

Louis Joliet and Father Jacques Marquette were commissioned by the French government in 1673 to set foot on the land. Father Marquette returned to the area one year later to establish an Indian mission. The first non-Indian to settle within Chicago's future boundaries was a Santo Domingan of mixed African and European ancestry, a trader named Jean Baptiste Point du Sable, a free black man apparently from Haiti, who came here in the late 1700s. He traded furs with the Indians on the north bank of the Chicago River, where he lived with his wife, Catherine, until 1796. He and his family then left with their children and moved to Peoria, Illinois. In 1795, the U.S. government built Fort Dearborn. It was burned to the ground by Native Americans in 1812, rebuilt and demolished in 1857. The 1832 Black Hawk War ended the last Native American resistance in the area. Chicago was incorporated as a town in 1833 and as a city in 1837, when its population reached four thousand.

A November 1836 committee applied to the state legislature for a city charter, and once the charter was approved, Chicago became a city. It had a population of 4,170 on March 4, 1837, and William B. Ogden served as the first mayor. Chicago was ideally situated to take advantage of immense trading possibilities newly created by the nation's westward expansion. Upon completion of the Illinois and Michigan Canal in 1848, a water link between the Great Lakes and the Mississippi River was created, but the canal was soon rendered obsolete by railroads. Today, 50 percent of rail freight still passes through Chicago, and it hosts one of the nation's busiest aviation centers, O'Hare and Midway International Airports. By the end of the 1850s, immigrants had poured into the city, drawn by jobs on the railroads that served the ever-growing agricultural trade. Twenty million bushels of produce were shipped through Chicago annually by then. The population topped 100,000.

Located smack in the center of the United States on the shores of Lake Michigan, Chicago is a vibrant, world-class city holding a rich history. Carl Sandburg's 1916 poem described it as "Hog Butcher, Tool Maker, Stacker of Wheat, Player with Railroads and Freight Handler to the Nation."

Nicknames ran from "Second City" to "Hog Butcher of the World," "Porkopolis," "Chi-town," "The Stinky Onion" and "White City." These nicknames stemmed from both the World's Columbian Exposition (the official shortened name of the World's Fair: Columbian Exposition, also known as the Chicago World's Fair, held in Chicago in 1893, celebrating the 400th anniversary of Christopher Columbus's arrival in the New World in 1492) and the White City (sometimes listed as White City Amusement Park) recreational area located in the Greater Grand Crossing and Woodlawn community areas on the south side of Chicago from 1905 until the 1950s. It was home of the first skyscraper, the ten-story Home Insurance Building designed by William LaBaron Jenney in 1884 and completed in 1885. The Sears Tower was once the world's tallest building until 1996, when Malaysia built the Petronas Towers.

Chicago's prime location in the middle of the country made it a favorite meeting spot, a legacy continuing into today. In 1860, the Republican Party

Chicago Art Institute, near the start of Route 66.

held its national political convention in Chicago and selected Abraham Lincoln, a lawyer from Springfield, Illinois, as its presidential candidate. As did many other Northern cities, Chicago profited from the Civil War, and this in turn boosted business in the burgeoning steel and tool-making industries. An abundance of freight was supplied for the railroads and canal. In 1865, the year the war ended, the Union Stockyards opened on the south side and profoundly affected the city for the next century.

Chicago's rail network and the invention of the iced refrigerator car opened the way for meat to be shipped long distances. The stockyards quickly became the major meat supplier to the nation, bringing great wealth to a few and jobs to many—as well as a major source of water pollution. In 1892, the first 3.6-mile elevated rail line was run by South Side Rapid Transit, running from the Congress Street terminal to Thirty-ninth Street. The line was extended to Jackson Park for the World's Columbian Exposition in 1893.

A superb location for the start of one of the most famous highways in America, just the name of the city conjures images of notorious dealings and mysterious happenings. A mere whisper of the strange events in the area is the 1955 discovery of the bodies of three nude, bound boys, found in a ditch in Chicago in the Robinson Woods (Robinson Reserve) area. Phantom voices, music reminiscent of Indian drumming, moans and the smell of lilacs in the dead of winter are associated with this location. Phenomena seem to revolve around the left side of the Robinson family monument, and no one can discover the cause. The House of Blues Hotel (formerly an office building, prior to Lowes hotels gutting and refurbishing it in 1998) in the landmark Marina City carries the odd stigma of having had a little girl die in the building, and it is said she now haunts the rooms. One visitor claimed his little boy heard a girl saying, "Want to play with me?" as her apparition played with his toys. Imprints of her small body appear in formerly unruffled sheets.

Between 1867 and 1890, newspapers reported numerous encounters with a sea serpent just off shore in Lake Michigan, with various sightings from Evanston down to Hyde Park. Described as bluish black with a grayish white underbelly, a long neck, a head about the same size as a human's and visible scales, the serpent was estimated between forty and fifty feet in length. People said it frequently bellowed like a bull. Fisherman Joseph Muhlke physically encountered the Lake Michigan monster in 1867, a mile and a half from shore, near Chicago's south side. He provided a detailed description and claimed that its head came within twenty feet of his boat.

Chicago has its share of otherworldly visitors. On November 7, 2006, federal authorities at Chicago O'Hare International Airport received a report that a group of twelve airport employees were witnessing a metallic, saucer-shaped craft hovering over gate C-17 at approximately 4:30 p.m. A dozen witnesses were observing a small, round disc-shaped object, metallic in appearance and visible for approximately two minutes. The UFO suddenly accelerated up through overcast skies, leaving behind a gaping hole of clear air in the cloud layer. The mysterious hole disappeared or closed within a few minutes.

TINLEY PARK LIGHTS

Reddish lights in a triangular formation were spotted at Tinley Park on three separate occasions in late 2004 and early 2005. Seen at low to intermediate altitude, the events produced multiple videos, photos and wide media coverage. Airspace near O'Hare International Airport was further occupied as the object(s) maneuvered slowly overhead. The incident was investigated by MUFON and featured on an episode of *UFO Hunters* on the Sci-Fi Channel.

THE GREAT FIRE OF 1871

With the growth of Chicago, its residents took heroic measures to keep pace, raising many of the streets five to eight feet to install a sewer system during the 1850s—and then they raised the buildings. Still recognized as a major disaster in the city's history, the wooden structures burned to the ground in the Great Chicago Fire of 1871 during a parched summer. The *Tribune* had reported a dry spell with less than three inches of rain between July and October that year, and then the unthinkable happened. On Sunday evening, October 8, 1871, shortly after 9:00 p.m., a fire broke out in the barn behind the home of Patrick and Catherine O'Leary at 13 DeKoven Street. Legend has it that a cow kicked over a lantern in a barn and started the fire, but Catherine O'Leary denied this charge. In fact, Chicago reporter Michael Ahern boasted about having fabricated the colorful tale. The true cause of the fire has never been determined for the event that left an area of about four miles long and almost a mile wide of the vulnerable Windy City, including its business district, in ruins.

Exhausted firefighters had not recovered from fighting a large fire the day before and were first sent to the wrong neighborhood. By the time they arrived at the O'Learys', they discovered the blaze had spread to the east and north.

Helping the fire spread was firewood in the tightly packed wooden buildings, ships lining the river, the city's elevated wood-plank sidewalks and roads and the commercial lumber and coal yards along the river. The size of the blaze generated extremely strong winds and heat, igniting rooftops far ahead of the actual flames. Wooden houses, along with commercial and industrial buildings, were consumed. The dry conditions and mostly wood buildings set the stage for a runaway conflagration, as a hot wind carried flaming embers across the city.

Primitive, horse-drawn firefighting equipment could do little to keep up with the spreading blaze, and soon almost every structure was destroyed or gutted in the area bounded by the river on the west, what's now Roosevelt Road to the south and Fullerton Avenue to the north. By 10:30 that evening, local firemen declared that the fire was out of control. Bystanders stated that "red rain" fell across the city. By midnight, the entire west side of Chicago had burned to the ground. As the fire raged through the central business district, it destroyed hotels, department stores, Chicago's city hall, the opera house and theaters, churches and printing plants. By 1:30 a.m., the fire had jumped the Chicago River and continued its hypnotic rampage, driving fleeing residents across the bridges. Mass panic ensued as the blaze jumped the river's north branch, burning through homes and a mansion on the city's north side. Residents fled to Lincoln Park and to the shores of Lake Michigan, where thousands sought refuge from the flames. Everything in its path, including the Tribune Building—believed to be fireproof—was destroyed. The fire continued through the city, and in the early morning hours, it destroyed the Water Works on Pine Street. The only thing that survived in that area was the Gothic stone water tower. An area four square miles, from Taylor Street to North Fullerton and Lake Michigan west to Halstead Street, ultimately became the charred wasteland left in the wake of the intense heat.

After two days, rain began to fall, and on the morning of October 10, 1871, the fire died out, leaving blackened puddles of devastation in the heart of the city. At least 300 people were dead, 100,000 people homeless and $200 million worth of property destroyed. The entire central business district of Chicago was leveled, marking the fire as one of the most spectacular events of the nineteenth century. The disaster prompted an outbreak of looting and lawlessness. Companies of soldiers were summoned to Chicago, and martial law was declared on October 11, ending three days of chaos. Martial law was lifted several weeks later.

The Chicago Fire Department training academy at 558 West DeKoven Street is on the site of the O'Leary property where the fire began. Amateur historian Richard Bales believed it was started by Daniel "Pegleg" Sullivan, who first reported the fire, because he ignited some hay in the barn while trying to steal some milk. Evidence reported in the *Chicago Tribune* by Anthony DeBartolo suggests Louis M. Cohn may have started the fire during a craps game. Cohn may also have admitted to starting the fire in a lost will, according to Alan Wykes in his 1964 book *The Complete Illustrated Guide to Gambling*.

A theory suggested in 1882 is that the Great Chicago Fire was caused by a meteor shower. At a 2004 conference of the Aerospace Corporation and the American Institute of Aeronautics and Astronautics, engineer and physicist Robert Wood suggested that the fire began when Biela's Comet broke up over the Midwest and rained down below. Four large fires on the same day on the shores of Lake Michigan might suggest a common root cause. Eyewitnesses reported sighting spontaneous ignitions, lack of smoke, "balls of fire" falling from the sky and blue flames. According to Wood, these accounts suggest that the fires were caused by the methane that is commonly found in comets.

As a side note, the Chicago City Council passed a resolution exonerating Catherine O'Leary, an Irish immigrant who died in 1895, and her cow.

Despite the fire's devastation, much of Chicago's physical infrastructure, plus St. Michael's Church, Old Town, Chicago Water Tower and its transportation systems, remained intact. Much of the debris from the fire was dumped into Lake Michigan as landfill, forming the underpinnings for Grant Park, Millennium Park and the Art Institute of Chicago. Twenty-two years later, Chicago celebrated its comeback by hosting the World's Columbian Exposition of 1893. One of the exposition buildings was rebuilt to become the Museum of Science and Industry. Refusing to be discouraged even by the Great Depression, in 1933 and 1934, the city held an equally successful Century of Progress Exposition on Northerly Island.

WATER TOWER

Myth and urban lore persist when even police officers are reported to have seen the ghost in the Chicago Water Tower and Pumping Station, a victim among the brave men who fought the blaze on October 10, 1871. Situated at Michigan and Chicago Avenues and due to its wonderful Joliet limestone and Gothic construction, the 154-foot-high water tower was one of the few buildings not destroyed in the fiery inferno. The water tower and water pump station across the street are two massive, castle-like structures standing out in downtown Chicago like Gothic cathedrals and the most iconic of Chicago's Lemont limestone structures, holding their own within the Magnificent Mile, that glorious, glamorous stretch of Michigan Avenue, which draws millions of sightseers from all over the world. In the midst of the glitz, the tower is a reminder of all that was lost in the fall of 1871 and what survives. Legend has it that during the fire, a man stayed behind in the tower instead of fleeing, tirelessly manning the pumps until he found that there was nothing more he could do. Rather than facing the fire, he ran up the stairs and hanged himself before the fire could get to him.

Paranormal researchers are reportedly uncertain about the origin of the apparition. It is thought that the phenomenon stems from the days after the fire, when Chicagoans lived under martial law. In the wake of the fire, looting and further burning became the order of the day, with an enforced curfew and a decree that all who did not answer to police would be shot—or hanged—immediately. Reports of strange lights at the top of the tower have

Vintage postcard of the water tower after the Chicago Fire.

been made, and no lights are near these windows. People passing by have also seen him swinging from a rope in front of the windows. The water tower marks the area of Chicago known as Streeterville, named for the explorer Captain John Streeter, who laid claim to the land only to have it taken from him by the city. The land fell beneath his furious curse, and some wonder if that was the reason for the sightings of the poor firefighter.

Since 1871, historians, journalists and others invested in Chicago's history have been confounded by the lack of historical documentation before the year of the fire. In fact, almost all of the city's historical records, public and private, were destroyed that October. From these letters sent abroad by survivors of the fire that today lie nestled safely with the Chicago Historical Society, it is apparent that many Chicagoans were shot and hanged in accordance with the temporary orders in place immediately after the fire. Possibly any ghosts at the structure could be tied to the chaos of those days, and it may be that the building's handsome limestone itself helps to harbor the memories.

One more ghost that exists due to the Great Fire is Father Damen, a Jesuit priest from Holland and founder of Holy Family Church, the second-oldest church in Chicago, with twenty-three priests, twenty-five thousand parishioners and five thousand students in his five grade schools, St. Ignatius High School and the college that became Loyola University of Chicago, all for the higher educations of boys. In October 1871, the ghosts of two drowned former altar boys appeared and predicted the fire, warning the church's parishioners that the horrific event was about to occur. Father Damen prayed that entire night, and the wind shifted from the southwest, pushing the flames to the east and away from the church, sparing it from the conflagration. Seven candles are kept lit in front of the picture of Our Lady of Perpetual Help in memory of that miracle. Rumors and legend hold that the church was built on the site of either an ancient Indian cemetery or an Indian battleground. Father Damen's ghost has been seen—dressed in clerical garb and also as a white, filmy spirit—at the Holy Family Church on West Roosevelt Road and at St. Ignatius College, just next door. Father Damen died far from Chicago on January 1, 1890, during his retirement in Nebraska at Creighton University.

Another Chicago fire and the resulting ghost tales from the deaths connected with it, that has become a thing of lore, occurred in the 1920s. Another grim prediction of the upcoming fire perhaps came when Francis (Frank) X. Leavey, resident at 6507 South Whipple and a thirteen-year veteran at Engine Company 107, said the prophetic words, "This is my last day with the department," as he leaned his soapy left hand against the window pane during spring cleaning. That winter had been bitterly cold, and the budding of spring came late. Now the dry conditions were taking their toll on the firefighters, making their mood somber and melancholy. At 7:30 p.m. on Good Friday, April 18, smoke was noticed pouring out of Curran's Dance Hall on Blue Island Avenue. The firebox lever of alarm box 372 was pulled by the witness, and a ticker-tape device dubbed "big joker" clicked out the message of the blaze two miles away from Engine Company 107 and Truck Company 12. The doomed Leavey (some spellings indicate Leavy) told his captain he'd finish the window after he returned.

Five squads raced to Curran's. The blaze was minor and well under control when the outer wall buckled. A cry went up, "Get out! Get out!" but the matchstick walls crumbled in a lethal embrace, trapping eight men. After the shower of debris had knocked out the electrical box, a portable light was brought in while firemen searched for their companions trapped beneath the rubble. Frank's face is said to have been the only recognizable one among the fatalities. Later investigation brought questions that Curran's Hall was torched deliberately.

The next day, one of the firemen noticed something strange about the window that Frank had been washing the day before. There seemed to be an unusual embedded stain on the glass, a "hand of Death" etched into the glass. No amount of scrubbing could remove the five-fingered mark, not even when ammonia was applied or when the firefighters went so far as to take razor blades to the glass to scrape the handprint away.

An expert from the Pittsburgh Plate Glass company brought a special chemical solution to the firehouse, guaranteeing that it would remove the print, but it, too, failed. Suggestions that the pane of glass be removed met with arguments, as the firemen stated it wasn't right to fool with the unknown. An official from the city even came with a fingerprint comparison, and the prints matched Frank's. For the next twenty years, the curse of the "telltale hand" defied all explanation and was a common attraction to visitors and other firemen from around the city, where it remained for twenty years. Finally, on the morning of April 18, 1944, exactly twenty years after Frank's death, a careless paperboy tossed the morning edition at the firehouse and shattered the window where Frank's handprint had been.

806 West Belmont: Victorian Antiques/That Steak Joynt/ The Adobo Grill/Piper's Bakery

During the Prohibition era, Chicagoans kept alcohol flowing in town as illegal speakeasies popped up in every neighborhood, hidden in basements, backrooms and soda shops. One of Capone's speakeasies was the home fated to become the now-closed Victorian House Antiques, built in 1879 at 806 West Belmont. A woman was murdered in this home in the 1880s, and four people later died in a fire in the attic rooms. Folks who've been in the attic area have reported feeling moving cold spots, doors opening and closing, shadowy figures, movement of objects and strange sounds. The shop had acquired two portraits from the Catherine and William Devine (a milk merchant in early Chicago) residence after it was razed. The owner of Victorian House Antiques, Al Morlock, hated the portraits and considered them to be bad luck. The woman's portrait gave him the creeps, and once when he was walking past them, it slipped from its hook, falling on his toe and breaking it. That was it; he wanted to either sell or burn them both. Along

Al Capone. *Drawing by Janice Tremeear.*

came Warren Black, the interior decorator for That Steak Joynt, located at the entrance to Piper's Alley, part of Old Town that was destroyed by the fire.

Originating as Piper's Bread Factory in the late 1800s and described as a major source of bread for the region as well as shipping across the United States, it has since hosted a series of businesses, both as That Steak Joynt and later the Adobo Grill, a Nuevo Latino restaurant. Built in 1872 by Henry Piper, the three-story building shared a wall with a comedy club, the Second City. When the great fire of 1871 tore through Chicago, Piper's Bakery burned to the ground. Henry Piper rebuilt an even more beautiful building, inside and out, to house Piper's Bakery, the right wall of which was attached to the shop next to it. On its left side, there was a winding alley next to Piper's Bakery, called Piper's Alley, a mecca for tourists and the "hip" generation. The neighborhood's pre-fire history can be seen in the winding layout of the streets in the Old Town Triangle Historic District. The urban flight of the 1950s saw many classic, Victorian-era structures converted into boardinghouses that became affordable for beatniks; artists, folk musicians, actors and others moved in and converted the alley into the counterculture capital of Chicago over the next two decades. The area became a major entertainment spot in the 1960s, and its stores included: The Man at Ease, Ripley's Believe It or Not Museum, a wax museum, the Pickle Barrel, the Crystal Pistol, John Brown's, the Sweet Tooth and many other unique shops, eating places and cabarets. On December 3, 1967, the *Chicago Tribune* wrote a description of Piper's Alley, saying, "Visitors enter under a gigantic lamp suspended over the sidewalk, [and then] walk east along a brick alley lined with carriage lamps."

After sixty years, Henry Piper retired in the 1920s. The ornate structural layout designed by Piper drew a variety of businesses throughout the twentieth century, including a laundry and a hardware store. The hand-

Piper's Alley. *Artwork by Robert Birkenes, used with permission from the artist.*

carved art, the glorious woodwork and sculptured baroque ceiling offered a most sought-after ambiance.

In 1962, this beautiful building was bought by Billy Siegel and Raudell Perez, for their new restaurant and bar, That Steak Joynt. They hired Warren Black to fill it with priceless antiques gathered from all over the city. Black desired antiques from the Victorian era for the steakhouse decor and had accumulated a crystal chandelier, busts of copper and bronze and a bust of a peasant holding a flask acquired from the defunct Matson Steamship Line. Add the lovely pieces left from the bread factory, and the location was nearly a mini-museum. The Devine portraits were perfect for his design and were placed on the wall of the staircase leading to the second-floor dining room. People passing the portraits soon reported a sudden chill in that spot, no matter the season. The chill was not felt every time someone would pass, but only at certain times. Catherine's portrait was said to been seen smiling if one looked at her face via the mirror hung on the opposite wall. The smile vanished when viewing the painting directly, but people swore they felt her eyes follow them up the stairs. This oil painting of the dead wife of a wealthy Chicago milk salesman would leave everyone who sat near it feeling frigid. Management had a problem keeping night help because many of the cleaning crew complained of singing, voices and dark figures throughout the building. Freshly extinguished candles could be smelled even though all candles lit were still burning, and boxes have been moved from place to place. A woman was seen walking to the stairs and vanishing.

The original bakery case, hand-carved from black walnut by artisans, was turned into a bar, and Siegel and Raudell Perez added a leaded-glass window for its shelves. The Matson bust was placed directly behind the bar, and its reputation for changing expressions and causing strange feelings when around it brought unease to the employees and customers. Unique powers were linked to the statue, including the ability to give tips on the stock market.

The restaurant had two floors connected by a Victorian-style staircase. There was a main dining room and bar area on the first floor, an upstairs dining room and a smaller, lower-level dining room. Throughout the restaurant, one would find many antiques, works of art and stained glass, all purchased from art dealers or from estates of homes in Chicago. The result was trendy and upscale, popular with those wanting an Old World, artistic, European experience. That Steak Joynt was the last of the Victorian bordello–style houses, with flocked walls, oil paintings and nude statuary.

Several well-publicized séances sparked notoriety, held upstairs in one of the dining rooms by notable psychics and attended by celebrities, including Mrs.

Jack Brickhouse. Unusual things occurred, including one newspaper reporter falling extremely ill. During the 1980s, local medium Robert Dubeil held regular séances, making contact with three entities: the architect who designed the building, a female customer of Piper's Bakery and an unknown male.

Workers who cleaned at night would refuse to come back, and unseen hands would shove bartenders and servers, according to their frantic claims. Shadowy figures were seen, and the sounds of singing came out of nowhere. Women visiting the restroom heard hard-heeled footsteps and the rustle of long skirts behind them; upon turning to see who was there, they found themselves alone in the bathroom. Lights were often seen near the bathroom, and the stall doors would shut without aid.

One barmaid was grabbed by an unseen force and dragged to a stairwell in a violent fashion while she was busing tables; the force on her wrist left white impressions in her skin. She was dragged, screaming, to the stairwell, and when the manager found her, she was laid out on the floor, with red finger welts on her wrist and the heel of her shoe broken.

Occurrences described in the building include creaking doors, disembodied voices, moans, footsteps and a bluish white mist forming behind the bust. On a paranormal investigation of the building, a photograph was taken of the bust (using special infrared film), and two white fingers of energy appeared, seemingly being generated by the marble statue. Cold spots, high-pitched squeals, growls and moving lights add to the strange magnetic readings captured on equipment by paranormal researchers. The kitchen door was seen swinging open, and a figure was spotted.

On April 6, 1991, a paranormal team and Celeste Busk of the *Chicago Sun-Times* stayed the night. Equipment and teams were set up in three areas: the main dining room/bar area, the upstairs dining room and the smaller lower-level dining room. Photographs reveal a glowing red light, a crescent-shaped white light, strange magnetic readings picked up in the dining room and the figure of what appeared to be a monk hovering over a table, though the middle section of his body was missing. (*Note*: Some accounts state the lower half of his torso was missing.) Thirty-five-millimeter photos taken of the peasant bust showed figures of bluish white lights.

On April 14, 1994, the team brought along Janet Davies from Channel 7 ABC Eyewitness News, and the night yielded sounds of a body being dragged across the floor, flickering lights, footsteps, cold spots, doors opening and closing on their own, strange noises on the stairs and the figure of a man without a middle sitting at a table that disappeared when approached. A camcorder mounted at the top of the stairs recorded a woman's moan, a high-pitched squeal and two guttural growling noises, which were also heard by the investigators. The scent of a burning odor and flowers occurred all night.

Two entities were seen together on the staircase, disappearing into thin air in the dining room. Patrons were touched or had someone unseen brush up against them. Cold spots followed them up the stairs. The bartender was adding up sales for the night when he saw two yellow eyes staring at him.

After Raudell Perez, who saw many of the paranormal events, died, the building was eventually sold to the Adobo Grill in 2000, another upscale restaurant with a bar, specializing in Mexican food. A visitor said of the place, "We heard noises all evening and had a shadow figure show up in a photo," though reports of hauntings diminished after the new ownership.

EASTLAND DISASTER HISTORIC SITE

Undoubtedly since the building of the famed Route 66, scores of fatal accidents have taken place that have not been documented. One of the worst accidents took place nine years before Route 66 was commissioned.

The passenger steamer SS *Eastland* was launched in 1903, designed to carry 650 passengers, but major construction and retrofitting in 1913 supposedly allowed the boat to carry 2,500 people. A naval architect warned officials that unless structural defects were remedied to prevent listing, a serious accident could occur.

About 7,300 Western Eclectic employees and their families arrived at 6:00 a.m. on July 24, 1915, at the dock between LaSalle and Clark Streets to be ferried to a company picnic in Michigan City, Indiana, via five steamers. As the line of passengers filed up the gangplank, Chief Engineer Joseph Erickson became concerned about his ship's demeanor. The *Eastland* was persistently more persnickety than usual on that morning, intent on leaning a bit to one side or the other even as the engine room crew pumped water into the ballast tanks to keep the ship and its shifting load on an even keel. At its capacity of 2,500, the gangplank was hauled, and the ship's orchestra began playing in the ballroom. Still dockside, passengers began their festivities with dancing, despite the overcrowded conditions or the slowly increasing slope of the dance floor. Some reports indicate that the crowd may have gathered on one side of the boat to pose for a photographer, thus creating an imbalance on the boat. Erickson opened one of the ballast tanks, which contained water within the boat to stabilize the ship, and the *Eastland* began tipping precariously. Reports say the crew of the boat jumped back to the dock when they realized what was happening. Immediate panic ensued with passengers trying to squeeze through portholes and jumping into the river to escape being crushed by the capsizing boat. Women with layers of heavy skirts were screaming for their children as they themselves were dragged to the river bottom by soaked clothing or other bodies. One female survivor who was forced beneath the water said she saw baby carriages on the river's bottom.

The *Eastland* slowly listed onto its port side in the Chicago River in less than fifteen minutes and in no more than twenty feet of water, entombing many. Between 800 to 850 men, women and children drowned. Rescuers quickly attempted to cut through the hull with torches, allowing them to pull out 40 people alive. Over the course of several days, the bodies were collected as police divers pulled up body after body, while thieves rummaged through the valuables of the dead, often stealing items directly from their bodies. Twenty-two entire families died in the tragedy. One diver broke down in a rage, and the city sent workers out with a large net to prevent bodies from washing out into the lake.

The *Chicago Tribune* stated on July 24, 1915, "844 people[…]were trapped or trampled below decks. Although most were young factory workers from Berwyn and Cicero, 21 entire families were wiped out."

A *Tribune* archive photo of the rescue was captioned: "The tugboat *Kenosha* served as a floating bridge to let survivors reach safety after the *Eastland* steamship disaster. As the ship was being cast loose from its moorings on the south bank of the Chicago River, the *Eastland* slowly settled on its side. The ship was in only 20 feet of water but that was deep enough to drown 844 people."

Years later, the *Tribune* of June 17, 2012, recalled the disaster: "A large crowd of horrified spectators watched as the S.S. *Eastland*—only a few feet from the shore of the Chicago River downtown—turned on its side…The Second Regiment Armory, on Washington Boulevard, served as a temporary morgue for victims, when the ship slowly settled on its side and 844 people drowned. Some people were never identified."

The *Eastland* was pulled up from the river, renamed the *Willimette* and converted into a naval vessel. It was turned into scrap following World War II. All lawsuits against the owners of the *Eastland* were thrown out by a court of appeals, and the exact cause of the tipping and subsequent disaster has never been determined. Months after the accident, rumors began that the ship itself was haunted by the dead.

Paranormal investigators and visitors alike often feel the area between the Clark and LaSalle Bridges is a hotspot for paranormal activity, with reports of bloodcurdling screams, cries of terror, moans and terrified calls for help. Orbs and misty figures appear in photographs taken at the spot in the river where the boat was docked that tragic day.

EXCALIBUR NIGHTCLUB

Excalibur Nightclub once hosted the Chicago Historical Society. When the *Eastland* disaster occurred in 1915, the bodies of many of the victims were brought to the Chicago Historical Society building, so it, too, temporarily served as a makeshift morgue. However, during the city's early years, the building burned down during the Great Chicago Fire. After reconstruction of the city began, the new structure became a church and then the Chicago Historical Society from 1892 to 1931. It then housed other tenants until it was finally reborn as a nightclub, the Limelight, in 1985. Shortly after opening, employees and patrons reported strange events and occurrences that could not be explained. Hauntings continue beyond the change from the Limelight to the three-story, sixty-thousand-square-foot Gothic graystone Excalibur, with its stately arched doorway framed by winged gargoyles and "Chicago Historical Society" etched into it. Architect Henry Ives Cobb drafted the structure in the Romanesque Revival style, erecting the roughly hewn granite building in 1892 as the second location for the Chicago Historical Society. The original building was supposedly fireproof but fell to the Great Fire; the caretaker barely survived by jumping out of the second-story window. Legend says he saw three women run inside just before the fire enveloped the building. Never seen again, they could be among the ghosts haunting the nightclub.

According to Joseph Kirkland's 1893 book, *The Chicago Massacre of 1812: With Illustrations and Historical Documents*, another ghost is that of Jean Lalime, whose skeleton was transported to the Chicago Historical Society and kept in the new building after he was killed by John Kinzie. The feud was sparked by Lalime's sympathizing with the Native Americans at the time. Lalime had been living in Du Sable's former home until Kinzie purchased it from Burnett. Lalime stayed at Fort Dearborn as a translator between the soldiers and indigenous populations and was a spy investigating corruption at the fort. A fight broke out between the two, and Kinzie stabbed Lalime with his own knife, buried his body two hundred yards to the west and tended to the grave for years out of guilt. Lalime's body was moved onto church grounds nearby by Kinzie or his sons. Years later, in 1891, Lalime's body was found by construction workers. The coroner's examination and consideration of the historical accounts determined the body to be that of Lalime, and it was put on display at the historical society.

Ghosts play here: glasses fall and shatter for no reason, employees hear their names being called with the voice resembling a known person from miles away, cold spots persist throughout the building, liquor bottles are smashed, people and shadow figures move about on the third floor, odd noises are heard, the specter of a woman is seen traveling the stairwell, beer bottles open by themselves, a little girl has been spotted laughing and wandering about at various hours of the day and screams come from the Dome Room, where a lawyer hanged himself. Howling and crying come from the upstairs bathroom, candles put out by the employees relight on their own and motion sensors and alarms go off by themselves.

While some reports maintain that the ghosts of the Excalibur are from the *Eastland*, others claim this is a myth; the bodies were never brought to this location. The club is now called the Castle and billed as Chicago's most haunted nightclub. On December 31, 2012, it merged with its sister nightclub, Vision, whose entrance was on the north side of the building.

Promotional postcard from Harpo Studios.

HARPO STUDIOS

Harpo Studios, formerly the Second Regiment Armory and the filming location of *The Oprah Winfrey Show* and *The Rosie O'Donnell Show*, was one of the makeshift morgues, as was the Reid Murdoch building on the river and a "floating morgue" underneath the Wells Street Bridge. Nearly two hundred dead were transported here as merchants loaned out wagons for the bodies and countless blocks of ice were brought in to keep the fallen cool until they could be identified by family members.

Renovated in the 1980s, the building is filled with mournful sobbing, whispers, old-time music and the marching footsteps of a large crowd. Doors slam shut, phantom laugher is heard and the "Gray Lady" is seen, even caught on the studio's security cameras. She wears a floor-length dress and old-fashioned hat of the type typically worn around 1915. One employee was frightened by the sounds of people outside her door, yet she was the only person on the floor. When a guard arrived, she said she'd opened her office door to see who was outside, and although no one could be seen, she continued to hear laughing and talking. A security guard who worked for Harpo for three years was quoted as saying, "I can say for sure that there are spirits walking the halls."

CEMETERIES

Rosehill Cemetery

Constructed of Joliet limestone in 1864 in an architectural style referred to as "castellated Gothic," the gate of the famously haunted cemetery mirrors the Gothic architecture of the water tower in Chicago. The site has been a backdrop for movie scenes such as the final fight scene in *Next of Kin*, filmed near the chapel, or copied as a set piece for the funeral scene in *Backdraft* to represent the Firefighter's Memorial in the movie. Rosehill contains remains of over 200,000 people, including many of the rich and elite of Chicago's past. Buried in its over 350 acres are famous Chicagoans like Aaron Montgomery Ward, Richard Warren Sears, Arthur Rubloff, Henry Crown, William Boyington (designer of the water tower), Charles Hull, John G. Shedd and sixteen Civil War generals and fourteen former Chicago mayors. Among the ghostly activity here, Sears is spotted in top hat and tails wandering near his burial vault. Civil War–era real estate tycoon Charles Hopkinson died in 1885 and was entombed in his crypt, resembling a miniature version of a Gothic cathedral. On the anniversary of his death, a gruesome moaning rose from the crypt, accompanied by the sounds of rattling chains.

A female specter dressed in a long gown and thought to be Carrie Kalbas was seen on October 1995 around 8:00 pm. near her unmarked grave. After floating in midair, the vision dematerialized into mist, frightening the poor groundskeeper. Her living niece contacted the cemetery the next day claiming Carrie had visited her, complaining she'd not been properly remembered. A monument was ordered for Carrie, who died on October 25, 1933, from coronary thrombosis at a hospital in Wheaton, Illinois.

A haunted statue within Rosehill belongs to Frances Pearce, who died at the age of twenty in 1864 (some reports say 1854) during childbirth (though some cases indicate from tuberculosis). Her infant daughter followed her to the grave only four months later. Her distraught husband, Horatio Stone, commissioned Chauncey Ives to sculpt a memorial of Frances and the child, immortalizing them in gorgeous, milky-white marble as a testament to his grief. Originally buried at the Old City Cemetery in Lincoln Park, Frances was later moved to Rosehill. The addition of a boxed-in glass enclosure to preserve it from the harsh Chicago weather was added shortly after its creation. According to legend, on the anniversary of her death, the glass container fills with a mysterious glowing white mist, and the statues rise up in greeting.

All in all, five ghosts are said to inhabit the cemetery, and it is forever linked to the Hull House demon baby tale via Charles Hull, builder of the haunted Hull House, who lies at Rosehill.

BACHELOR'S GROVE

According to a legend, black magic and occult rituals were once practiced at Bachelor's Grove around the grave marked "Infant Daughter," and now gifts and trinkets are left in hopes of bringing good luck. Bachelor's Grove Cemetery (formerly known as Everdon's) in Midlothian, Illinois, is believed to have opened in 1843–44. The first documented burial was of Elizabeth Scott. The last known funeral service took place here in 1965, and after the last internment of the ashes of Robert Shields in 1989, the cemetery has long since been abandoned. It's the site of over one hundred different accounts of strange phenomena, apparitions, unexplained sights and sounds and glowing balls of light. Renamed Bachelor's Grove in mid-1800, the true origins of the name remain uncertain, although two popular theories exist. One says the area was inhabited by unmarried male German immigrants who found employment constructing the Illinois-Michigan Canal, hence the name Bachelor's Grove. A second thought is that Bachelor's Grove was named for the Batchelder family settlers in 1845. But no historical records give support to this theory other than old cemetery records that spell Bachelor's with a *T*, a German spelling, accepted by most historians as the official, authentic spelling of the cemetery name.

Until the late 1960s, the main thoroughfare leading to the cemetery was part of the turnpike of the city. After the road closing, the small area gained its reputation for ghostly activity. Isolation gave the cemetery an attraction for young couples to seek privacy, and apparently the young men found opportunities to tell their girlfriends tales about the ghosts of the cemetery and the small lagoon across from it.

Like many "forgotten" cemeteries, Bachelor's Grove lacked any true preservation attempts, and vandalism caused the destruction and loss of over 150 tombstones. Now in the middle of a forest preserve, possibly only 10 tombstones remain at their original locations. Bodies have also been relocated, increasing the difficulty of knowing the exact number of people buried there.

The Fulton family plot features in one of the main stories, with a mother seen walking through the area mourning her dead baby. Some cases tell of the Madonna or white lady seen carrying the lifeless infant. She is thought to be a Mrs. Rogers (possibly Luella Fulton Rogers, wife of Daniel W. Rogers, but Luella died at age sixty-five). She's also thought to be the woman in a famous photo, sitting atop the "quilted" tombstone. She wasn't visible to the eye when her image was captured in 1991, and there's no explanation for the woman's identity, but she appears to be mourning. Other pictures have been dubbed "fairy photos" for the oddly colored spheres that appear to be moving through the graveyard.

In the 1870s, a farmer was pulled into this pond by his horse. The animal drowned beneath the weight of the plow, and the farmer, entangled in the reins, sank with it. More than a century later, forest rangers have spotted the phantom farmer being pulled to his death. The pond/lagoon is rumored to be a dump site for Chicago mobsters. The most famous lagoon story involves Al Capone, who owned a house a few blocks from Bachelor's Grove and disposed of his victims here; it's said the souls of those he murdered linger to this day.

Out of about eighty reported ghosts, a small boy has been heard crying, vocal recordings of a young girl have been caught near the grave of one of the Fultons and there is video footage of shadows running by some visitors. A child specter is seen running across a bridge at the pond, and darkly hooded figures are spotted.

A lamp-lit ghost house lies within the woods and has even been captured on film, but it disappears as one approaches. (A similar urban legend exists in Rolla, Missouri, along old Route 66. This one says you can come upon a tomb that disappears.) However, no such building ever existed. Phantom cars are seen moving around the cemetery, another mirror tale of an event in Rolla. At times, the ghostly lights appear to be red, bouncing in the woods at rapid speeds or zipping through the air to show up on film as orbs. One of the stranger tales is of a two-headed man walking in the woods outside of the cemetery. Blue orbs are seen, as well as white mists and a glowing yellow man who lurks about, often wearing a yellow suit and then vanishing in a "sparkling" manner. In one account, a tree was shaking when this yellow ghost left. Police patrolling the area have documented their personal experiences of apparitions, ghostly lights and transparent cars and car accidents along the turnpike.

A visitor to the site never feels entirely alone, and one of the more frequent sightings is of phantom monks, the alleged guardians of the grove. Other rumors revolve around a satanic cult plying the dark arts inside the cemetery. Visitors claim they've been clawed and bitten, attacked by spirits unhappy over the disrespect of the desecration within the sacred grounds.

"Resurrection Mary"/O'Henry's Roadhouse

One cannot recount tales of the ghosts of Chicago without telling the story of "Resurrection Mary." It's said that since Mary's grave was found, she no longer haunts the area connected with Resurrection Cemetery, from which she earned her nickname. However, tales of her reappearance are popping up once more. She is said to be a most beautiful ghost: blue eyed, flaxen-haired and in her late teens. She's elusive, and on the rare occasions she allows herself to be seen, she's wearing her long, off-white ball gown, with a shawl and dancing shoes. Suspicions are that she was going to the Roadhouse, which has since been the home of the establishments Oh Henry's Roadhouse, O'Henry's 2, Cavallone's West, Rico D's, Frankie's Roadhouse, Willowbrook Ballroom, the Stag's Head and now the Irish Legend. The ghost is thought to be Mary Bregavy (although she had dark hair, not flaxen), a member of Chicago's Polish immigrant community who had gotten into a fight with her boyfriend at the ballroom in 1934. Attempting to hitchhike home, she was struck by a car and killed. Her identity might instead be that of Mary Miskowski, killed as she was crossing the street to go to a costume party. Anna Mary Norkus is another candidate for Mary. She'd convinced her father to take her to the O'Henry Ballroom on her thirteenth birthday. While driving home, the car overturned, killing the young girl. Mary might be nothing more than an urban legend and is merely Chicago's form of the "vanishing hitchhiker," ghost stories spawned by the onset of the automobile. The tales vary but have oddly interlocking similarities in which a person is seen alongside the road, attempting to hitchhike. After a motorist gives the hitchhiker a ride, he or she is surprised to discover the passenger has vanished from the car.

Mary is best known for jumping on the running boards of cars in 1939, attempting to hitch rides to the Willowbrook Ballroom. She would dance all night with the single males, none of whom recognized her as a ghost. Her manner was aloof and her skin icy cold to the touch. She'd ask for rides after the dance, requesting to go north on Archer Avenue, and always disappeared as the car reached Resurrection Cemetery, where her grave is thought to be.

One night in 1936, young man named Jerry Palus danced with Mary at a local establishment called the Liberty Grove Hall and Ballroom, not the usually reported location of the Willowbrook Ballroom. He even kissed her, reporting that her lips were cold and clammy. She said she lived on Damen Avenue, but once he started to drive her home she directed him to the cemetery in the opposite direction. Mary suddenly asked Jerry to stop the car, and she then hurriedly exited the vehicle. She crossed Archer Avenue and disappeared into the closed gates of Resurrection Cemetery. When he saw her vanish, he knew he'd danced with a specter. The next day, he tracked down the address, and the woman who answered the door and his questions about Mary lamented the loss of her daughter years ago, the victim of a hit-and-run driver while coming home from a night of dancing. He noticed a portrait on the coffee table of the dead daughter, and she matched the girl Jerry had danced with at the ballroom.

Mary traveled as well. In 1973, a girl fitting her description was seen at Harlow's on Cicero on the southwest side of town. Bouncers checked the IDs of everyone who entered, but no one saw her come in or leave though she was seen dancing alone at the establishment on two separate occasions. That same year, a cab driver came into Chet's Melody Lounge, across the street from Resurrection Cemetery, inquiring about a young lady who had left without paying her fare.

Kim DeWitt of ParaNatural Research Association has a personal story about Mary. Her family relates the tale of how her grandfather, who was a Yellow Cab driver, and her grandmother, who served as a cocktail waitress at the then country club, both encountered the girl who may be the hitchhiking ghost. Kim says, "She frequented the speakeasy/club [Kim paused here and gestured with her hand to indicate the ambiguity of the establishment] and was at a debutante dance waiting for her fiancé. My grandfather took the girl in his cab, and my grandmother served her drinks."

Sightings continued in 1976, 1978, 1980 and 1989, with Mary passing through cars or exiting a vehicle without opening the doors. Other reports have Mary darting out of the cemetery in front of oncoming cars. She is struck down with a solid thud, but when drivers stop to help, she is gone. Also in 1976, a motorist reported what appeared to be a young girl locked inside the cemetery. At 10:30 p.m., Sergeant Pat Homa responded to the call, and in the illumination from his flashlight through the cemetery bars into the darkened burial grounds, no girl was found. However, two of the gate's bars were bent apart at sharp, weird angles. They appeared to have been bent apart by human hands. Examining the bars closer, he found impressions of small handprints and scorch marks appearing to be skin texture seared by incredible heat into the green patina of the metal. Metallurgist experts could not explain how the bars were bent. These supernatural marks of the small hands became big news, and curiosity-seekers thronged to see them. Hoping to discourage the crowds, cemetery officials attempted to remove the marks with a blowtorch, succeeding only in making them worse. The bars were cut off and sent away to be straightened. The gates were reinstalled in the early 1980s with the same bars; however, they were refitted upside down.

It's thought the connection to Native American land might be the cause for the paranormal activity in this location. Willow Springs can be found about twenty miles south of Chicago, in the Des Plaines River Valley, on an upland moraine formed by Ice Age glaciers and known for its beauty and ravines. Geologists refer to it as Mount Forest Island. In 1883, the railroad traveled south from Chicago to Willow Springs. The woods and surrounding land where this building sits include Chief Cagmega's Ridge, and Potawatomi Ridge Trail lies behind it. Archer Avenue runs in front of the building and was an Indian trail. Directly north of Willowbrook is the Des Plaines River. Fur trading between the Native Americans and the French traders took place here, and less than a mile northeast lies Native American healing waters. By 1883, railroad travel south from Chicago to Willow Springs was a reality. From 1892 to 1899, the construction of the I&M Canal brought more people as well, many of them Italians, adding to the growing numbers of Germans, Poles and Irish who called the place home. Ice harvesting off the river became a large moneymaking endeavor for the people living here.

An old saying goes, "Many owners have come and gone, but the spirits will remain." Founded in 1921 as an outdoor dance hall, owner John Verderbar grew his O'Henry Park throughout the 1920s until 1930, when disaster struck and the complex burned to ground-level ruins. Complete with restaurant, soda fountain and flower shop. The O'Henry Ballroom rose from its ashes like a Phoenix at the then staggering amount of $100,000. The 1930s and '40s found hundreds of thousands in the mood to swing, as the ballroom touched many lives since its construction in 1939 and became home to the biggest and best bands of the day. Count Basie's high-energy sounds, along with the oscillating rhythms of Benny Goodman, gave way to the infectious tempos of present-day swing groups like the Brian Setzer Orchestra or Big Bad Voodoo Daddy, and the site now hosts the big-band event Swingfest.

By the 1950s, lounges, restaurants and the elegant two-hundred-seat Willowbrook Room were added. Confusion grew between the O'Henry Ballroom and its popular Willowbrook Room. Eventually, the entire complex simply became known as the Willowbrook. A 1920s-style awning sat above the front door of a bar and dining room on the main floor.

A tale circulates that during the 1920s and '30s, a hapless bartender fell in love with one of the prostitutes, who was desired by a gangster. The gangster broke the bartender's neck, ambushing him as he came down the basement steps to get supplies. The gangster then beat the prostitute very badly, possibly to her death. It is thought that both were buried in the dirt basement. Her bloodied, pulverized face has appeared on occasion in the mirror of the bathroom.

Cold spots are felt, and rumors persist of an odd, almost perfect outline of a body on the floor of a secret room and what appears to be old blood vainly washed from the wall. Photos show a string of small red, triangular lights crossing from one side of the room to another, lights that were not there when the pictures were taken. A female entity appeared in front of the owner of Rico D's (the former O'Henry's) and conducted a conversation explaining how much she liked the improvements to the building. A shadow man wearing an overcoat is reported going up the stairs by employees.

JANE ADDAMS HULL HOUSE MUSEUM

Often rumors can affect the lives of people in negative ways. The same can be said for rumors of hauntings at locations, like the tale of the Devil Baby at

Hull House. Images of hooded monks only add to the legends coming from behind the doors of the Hull House.

Constructed by wealthy real estate developer Charles J. Hull at Halsted and Polk Streets in 1856 at a time when this was one of the most fashionable sections of the city, Hull House was never intended to become known as one of the most haunted locations in Chicago. Hull's wife died in the second-floor bedroom, and a few months later, it was reported that her ghost had begun haunting the room. Once the Hulls vacated the house, a Catholic convent, the Little Sisters of the Poor, operated a home for the elderly before Jane rented the building. Overnight guests began having their sleep disturbed by footsteps and what were described as "strange and unearthly noises." There were suspicions of the attic being haunted, and residents living on the second floor would leave a pitcher of water on the stairs leading to the attic in the belief that the ghost would not pass through water. Despite the rumors of the ghost, Jane moved into the Hull House on September 18, 1889, when the owner, Helen Culver, allowed rental of the house.

Laura Jane Addams was born to Sarah Weber Addams and John Addams on September 6, 1860, the same year in which Abraham Lincoln ran for president. Jane's father and Lincoln were good friends, and letters came addressed to Addams as "My Dear Double D—ed Addams."

The Chicago Fire of 1871 prompted the move of the upper class to other parts of the city, leaving the Near West Side to attract a large immigrant population of Italian, Greek and Jewish settlers. Surrounded by factories and tenement houses, the Hull House became one of the most famous places in Chicago by the 1880s. Jane Addams and Ellen Gates Starr in 1889 established it as a settlement house, providing education and services to help the city's working class and new European immigrant class. Jane Addams was born and raised in the village of Cedarville as the privileged daughter of a wealthy merchant. Tragedy visited her with the death of her father, occurring the same year she graduated from the Rockford Female Seminary. Falling into a deep depression and unsure what to do with her life, she spent a portion of her inheritance traveling in Europe. It would be in London, in the terrible slums of Whitechapel, where she would find her calling. She became the "voice of humanity" on the west side, enriching the lives of many unfortunate people at Hull House. The house and its workers sparked many reformations in Chicago.

By 1907, the converted 1856 Hull mansion had expanded to a massive thirteen-building complex covering nearly a city block with a gymnasium, theater, art gallery, music school, boys' club, auditorium, cafeteria, residences for working women, kindergarten, nursery, libraries, post office, meeting/club rooms, art studios, kitchen, dining room and apartments for the residential staff contained within its walls. Thousands of people from the surrounding neighborhood visited Hull House each week as the expanded complex provided space for the settlement's artistic, social and—first and foremost—educational programs. The Hull House charter read that its purpose was "to provide a center for a higher civic and social life, to institute and maintain educational and philanthropic enterprises, and to investigate and improve the conditions in the industrial districts of Chicago."

In *Return to the Scene of the Crime*, author Richard Linberg tagged the dark neighborhood near Hull House as the "darkest corner of Chicago." Criminals from around the city sought refuge on the west side, attracting the "lowest of the lowly" hoodlums. The district was awash in vice, with crooked cops and politicians collecting graft from brothels strung from Monroe and Lake Street, saloons, dope peddlers and all-night "druggists," who peddled their wares of cocaine, laudanum and over-the-counter medicines spiked with opium in this violent section of town along Sangamon, Green, Peoria, Curtis, Carpenter and Morgan Streets.

Addams was a persuasive and eloquent writer. Over the course of her lifetime, she published eleven books and hundreds of articles addressing the pressing issues of her time. Through her writing, she was able to convey the details of neighborhood life in a way that gave dignity to the human dramas she encountered. The uncanny episode of the Devil Baby became a way to discuss the plights of immigrants in the community and deal with issues of gender, aging, poverty, folklore and memory. In Jane's book, *Twenty Years at Hull House*, she talked about the ghost haunting the location. When Jane took over Hull House, several years had passed since the death of Mrs. Charles Hull. This didn't stop the persistent ghost from making her presence known. Mrs. Hull's

Hull House vintage collectible card.

bedroom was first occupied by Jane, who awoke one night to the sound of loud footsteps in the empty room. After repeated nights of this, she confided her story to Ellen, who admitted to experiencing the same sounds. Jane vacated the room, leaving it to whatever spirits resided there. The workers kept a bucket of water on the stairs, believing that the ghost was unable to cross over it. The spirit appeared sad but never caused any harm.

Jane would not be alone in noticing the unusual happenings. Helen Campbell, author of the book *Prisoners of Poverty*, reported seeing an apparition standing next to her bed after taking up Jane's offer to stay in the haunted room. When she lit the gas jet, the figure vanished. Mrs. Louise Bowen, a lifelong friend of Jane's; Mary Smith; and even Canon Barnett of Toynbee Hall, who visited the settlement house during the Columbian Exposition in 1893, also observed the strange and peculiar sounds and figures. Even modern-day visitors have reported feeling uncomfortable while touring the museum.

Perhaps the best story of Hull House was the inspiration for Ira Levinson's 1967 novel *Rosemary's Baby*, in which a young woman gives birth to the devil's child. In 1913, crowds of women descended on Hull House demanding to see a so-called Devil Baby. The perplexed and surprised Addams explained over and over again that there was no such baby in the house, but still the visitors came.

The Demon Baby is an urban legend, carrying with it one hundred variations. It is thought to have its roots in the statements made by a couple different men, and one version dealt with a pious Italian girl married to an atheist (some stories say she was Catholic). Apparently, when the young woman hung a picture of the Virgin Mary in the house, her husband vehemently tore it down from the bedroom wall, stating that he would rather have the devil himself in the house than the picture. The devil then incarnated himself in her coming child. Immediately after the birth, the Devil Baby ran about the table, shaking his finger in deep reproach at the father. The baby had pointed ears, horns, scale-covered skin and a tail. After enduring numerous indignities because of the child, the father fearfully brought him to Jane Addams at Hull House. In spite of the baby's shocking appearance, the residents wished to save his soul and brought him to church for baptism. They discovered the shawl wrapped around the child was empty, and the Devil Baby, fearing the holy water, ran lightly over the backs of the pews, dancing and laughing.

An Irish retelling of the legend claims the mother confessed to a priest about her affair with a man before her marriage, and her punishment was bearing the devil's baby.

A Jewish version (with variations) said the father of six daughters had said before the birth of a seventh daughter that he swore he'd rather have a demon child than another girl to disturb his peace, whereupon the Devil Baby promptly appeared. One variation states that two young women went to see *Faust*, and the woman who was due to give birth stared too intently at the stage devil, causing her child to be born in the image of Mephistopheles. Another legend states that the youngest daughter of a pious Jewish family married a Gentile without permission of her parents. Her enraged father declared he'd rather have the devil as a grandchild than a Gentile as a son-in-law, thus dooming his daughter to bear the Demon Baby. Another version states that the Devil Baby was caused by the lie of a woman who bore a child out of wedlock. When asked if her new baby was her first, her lie caused the child to be Satan.

Odd tales related to the child include it driving away from Hull House in a red automobile with a cigar in some versions that the newborn eagerly snatched from his father's lips. Another rumor says the devil was born around the Levy district and dropped off at Hull House. It's highly possible the baby was a deformed infant, and the mother felt she couldn't care for the baby. Not knowing what else to do with the child, Jane kept it locked in the attic of the house, where it later died. Legends persisted about a deformed boy hidden away in the upper floors of the building (a mirror story to the boy hidden in the attic of the haunted Lemp Mansion in St. Louis, also near Route 66—see my book *Missouri's Haunted Route 66: Ghosts Along the Mother Road*), and on certain nights, he's seen staring from the attic windows.

Jane Addams saw a quality of redemption in the tale of the Demon Baby. The elder women used the fable to ease memories of their own losses and sufferings, and women brought bullying husbands to see the child that resulted from a man's ill behavior toward his wife. Dysfunctional males could become hobos or hermits and society would leave them alone, but the times in which the Devil Baby was born were often brutal for women and children who might find themselves locked away in asylums, deemed "possessed" if their behavior was out of line. Women could become the victims of sexism, beaten if they raised their voices against their husbands or incarcerated against their will by irate husbands or male family members for not being obedient enough or for the mere act of holding liberating views or merely exhibiting behavior that deviated from the norms of their day. An unmarried woman who bore a child was at a greater risk of being institutionalized to avoid the embarrassment of her family. One might find herself and her child hidden away from public view by being committed into an asylum. The book *Women of the Asylum* tells the stories of women committed because they were "inconvenient," depressed or "in the way" or because they questioned the authority of their husbands, suffered from alcoholism or menopause or simply weren't good enough housekeepers. Often an "upstanding" husband seeking a new wife would place the first wife in the lunatic asylum and simply write the word "lunacy" on the admission form. He would then file for divorce, and a few months later, his marriage records to a much younger bride usually showed up. The original wife had done nothing wrong but grow older. The husband might say that his wife or child had died, and he could even have an obituary printed.

For the immigrant women in Chicago, the existence of the Demon Baby was a reminder of the ways of the Old World and was perfectly natural to believe in as their cornerstone of life revolved around religion, traditions and superstition. They made the pilgrimage with families in tow to see the child; this was a great adventure, a break in the sequestered routine of the pattern of life expected from them and a way to branch out from their reality without the penalty of lunacy falling upon them.

Jane Addams said, "During the weeks of excitement…it was the old women who really seemed to have come into their own, and perhaps the most significant result of the incident was the reaction of the story upon them. It stirred their minds and memory as with a magic touch, it loosened their tongues and revealed the inner life and thoughts of those who are so often inarticulate. They are accustomed to sit at home and to hear the younger members of the family speak of affairs quite outside their own experience in a language they do not understand." Addams also said, "Many of them who came to see the Devil Baby had been forced to face tragic experiences, the powers of brutality and horror had had full scope in their lives and for years they had had acquaintance with disaster and death."

The Hull House closed unexpectedly in January 2012, and since then, efforts have been in place to reopen it. One plan was to make it into a theater and apartment complex, but efforts in that arena failed. Petitions are underway to save the building. Before its closing, tours given on-site had guests reporting babies crying inside the garden and shutters opening and closing. Reports of a portal to hell or a hidden graveyard are said to be false, but the location is thought to have once been the site of a brothel and funeral parlor.

SITE OF ST. VALENTINE'S DAY MASSACRE

Clark Street bears an infamous history due to the horrific capsizing of the *Eastland* on the Chicago River and the legacy of the Mafia. When the *Eastland* capsized, the cleanup and burials of the 844 victims took weeks, leaving the dead to foul the muggy summer air as bodies decayed before identification and burials could take place.

On Valentine's Day during Prohibition in 1929, two bootlegging gangs played out a brutal scene that was an earmark of the warfare and gang-style murders that occurred between 1920 and 1930, resulting in more than five hundred deaths. The massacre at a garage on 2122 North Clark was the most spectacular of these events when seven of George "Bugs" Moran's men were gunned down in a rain of ninety bullets at close range from five men dressed in police uniforms and bearing sawed-off shotguns, a revolver and machine guns. Moran narrowly escaped having witnessed the black Cadillac touring car (like the type police used, complete with siren, gong and rifle rack) pull up and the "police" go inside the SMC Cartage Co. garage where Moran conducted his illegal business. "Bugs" left the scene before six of his men, including Frank

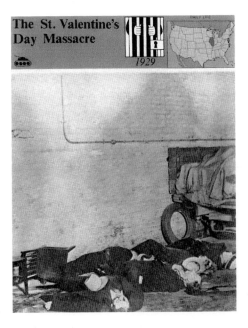

"Hock" Gusenberg (Moran's enforcer); his brother, Peter "Goosy" Gusenberg; and a German shepherd, lay dead. One man, gravely wounded by fourteen bullets in his body, muttered to the police, "Nobody shot me." He was hauled off to the nearest hospital, where he lived for another three hours.

Investigators thought the Detroit, Michigan "Purple Gang" was responsible. Moran believed Alphonse "Scarface Al" Capone's gang were the culprits, "because only the Capone gang kills like that." At the time, Al Capone ruled the south side, and Dion O'Bannon held reign over the north side. The papers did their best to show the

St. Valentine's Day Massacre vintage collectible card.

bullet-ridden bodies (some missing half their heads) in print from Cairo to Rockford, Illinois. Capone—America's Public Enemy No. 1—proved he was in Florida at the time of the massacre.

The garage was torn down, and brain-splattered, bloodied bricks from the north wall were used in a men's restroom, right behind the urinals, at a '20s-themed restaurant in Canada. One man intended to make the bricks morbid souvenirs of the shooting and sold them as keepsakes of the massacre sometime in the '70s. He claimed they were cursed and ruined his life, and many were returned due to the curse and bad luck associated with them. Each brick sold for a high price and held a paper of authenticity. This might be an example of objects being haunted by the victims of the St. Valentine's Day Massacre.

The city planted five trees to commemorate the location of that wall, and the area is now a lawn for a neighboring nursing home. Claims that the location is haunted are fueled by late-night visitors who hear the rapid fire of old-fashioned machine guns and men screaming or experience an intense sense of dread and fear. Dogs are known to react negatively to the area, cowering, running in fear and barking loudly at something that isn't there. The German shepherd shot on-site is said to haunt the area, and residents of the nursing home witness unusual lights and mists. One woman met with a phantom gangster in her room, randomly appearing wearing a fedora hat and double-breasted pinstriped suit.

As a side note: the entity of Moran's brother-in-law James Clark immediately began haunting Capone, who was living in his Florida house at the time of the massacres. From May 1929 to March 16, 1930, Capone spent eight months in the Eastern State Penitentiary after being arrested and imprisoned for carrying a concealed weapon. After his release, he attempted in vain to send the entity to the other side via a medium in 1931.

After his trial on October 18, 1931, Capone was convicted on the charge of tax evasion in 1925, and on November 24, he was sent to Atlanta to begin his eleven-year sentence. Word spread that Capone had taken over in Atlanta, and in 1934, he was transferred to Alcatraz. During his time of isolation, he complained of a ghostly visitor. "It looks like Alcatraz has got me licked," Capone stated.

In 1938, he was transferred to Terminal Island Prison in Southern California to serve out the remainder of his sentence and was released in November 1939. Broken in mind and spirit, Capone returned to Florida, as he had become mentally incapable of returning to gangland politics.

After a 1946 examination, both his physician and a Baltimore psychiatrist concluded that Capone had the mental capacity of a twelve-year-old child. Capone complained that the ghost plagued him, and the entity continued to haunt him until he died on January 25, 1947, in his Palm Island mansion from complications of syphilis.

Capone's valet driver reported seeing an apparition of Clark one time, and Capone himself could often be heard yelling at Jimmy to leave him alone. Capone was interred at Mount Carmel Cemetery in Illinois, where his ghost can sometimes be seen at his family's plot. Capone is also rumored to haunt his former cell at Alcatraz, where banjo music is heard. One of the ghosts residing at Eastern State is thought to possibly be Capone as well, visiting his cell, which was once decked out with expensive furniture, rugs and wall hangings.

SITE OF FORT DEARBORN

The name "Checaugou"—meaning wild onions—was given to the area around the Chicago River's mouth by the Potawatomi Indians. Part of the 1795 Treaty of Greenville gained the U.S. government a parcel of land at the mouth of the Chicago River. Strategically located, this portage area grew with the acquisition of the Louisiana Territory in 1803. Captain John Whistler arrived in Chicago to build a fort on the south side of the river, named after Henry Dearborn, President Thomas Jefferson's secretary of war. To the south of the fort sat homes and businesses; to the north of the river, John Kinzie and other traders lived with ties to the British, French and Indians.

Two hundred years ago, with the national government a mere twenty-three years old by 1812, the small fort at Chicago was the westernmost U.S. outpost on the Great Lakes, with fewer than five thousand settlers occupying the area. It was surrounded by hundreds of thousands of acres of prairie and woodland and populated by roving bands of Native Americans, including the Potawatomi, Shawnee, Miami, Ojibwa, Winnebago and others. By 1808, the fort had risen on a small hill overlooking the river. With William Henry Harrison campaigning against the local natives beginning in 1811, Indians began siding with the British. Growing resentment of the Potawatomi, incited by their leaders and Shawnee chieftain Tecumseh, led to a slaughter of settlers in 1812 at what is now Eighteenth and Calumet. ("Calumet" is French for the long-stemmed ceremonial tobacco pipes utilized by Native Americans, commonly known as peace pipes.)

Sometimes known as the Battle of Fort Dearborn, the massacre occurred after commander Captain Nathan Heald, under the orders of General William Hull, ordered an evacuation of the fort manned by fewer than sixty soldiers. Heald is said to have promised the Indians food, calico and other provisions of the fort but then changed his mind, fearing the weapons and alcohol would only inflame them and give them cause and means to take action against the settlers. Instead, he ordered all whiskey and gunpowder to be destroyed so it would not be seized for the British by the Indians. General Hull had heard of the fall of Fort Mackinac with its seventy-nine-man garrison and feared Dearborn would suffer the same fate. On August 14, Potawatomi chief Mucktypoke, called "Black Partridge," warned Heald that there would be an attack, and on August 15, the column of residents left Dearborn, even though the consensus had been to stay within the walls of the fort for safety.

Heald could not disobey his commanding officer, and the forced march to Fort Wayne ensued as a column of fifty-five soldiers, twelve civilian militiamen, nine women and eighteen children were led by former Miami warrior Billy Wells, who had a mythic stature on the U.S. frontier. Wells was

FORT DEARBORN, IN 1830.

Fort Dearborn.

born white but was raised to become Little Turtle's son-in-law and fought on the Miami side in the defeat of St. Clair in Ohio. Under his influence and with his face painted black as a sign he expected an ambush, more than thirty Miami warriors agreed to accompany the group. Less than two miles from the fort, Chief Blackbird and over five hundred Potawatomi and Winnebago ambushed the fort's residents from a nearby dune. Wells and Heald led a desperate attack, leaving the wagon train of women and children unprotected. The Miami warriors fled before the strength of the other tribes, the local militia was wiped out and half the soldiers were killed. Twelve children were beheaded by a young warrior who slipped into their covered wagon—"for which he was hated by the tribe ever after," said Simon Pokagon, son of a Potawatomi leader—and Mrs. Heald's black slave, Cicely, was one of two women killed while fighting to save the children. Margaret Helm, the wife of the fort's lieutenant, was saved by Black Partridge. Rebekah Heald, Nathan's wife, was wounded but survived.

"Wells fought one hundred or more single-handed, on horseback," wrote Pokagon, whose father was there, "shooting them down on right and left, in front and rear, until his horse fell under him and he was killed." Wells was scalped, his head cut off and his heart eaten by the chiefs to gain courage from consuming his body. Heald was wounded, and support arrived from Fort Wayne, Indiana, led by Heald's wife's uncle, Captain Hull. The battle lasted a mere fifteen minutes.

Lieutenant Linai Helm wrote a firsthand account of the scene after the massacre, noting, "When we arrived at the bank and looked down on the sand beach I was struck by the horror of men, women, and children lying naked with principally all their heads off."

Survivors were captured to sell to the British as slaves and were eventually ransomed back to their families. The fort was burned to the ground, and the Potawatomi denied any responsibility, instead placing blame on the Winnebago Indians. Different versions of what happened to the Miami escort with William Wells report that they either fought alongside the Americans or retreated when the fighting started. William Henry Harrison claimed the Miami fought against the settlers; he used the killings as an excuse to attack Miami villages, which led Chief Richardville and Pacanne to side with the British during the war.

Soldiers arriving at Chicago to rebuild Fort Dearborn four years later found bones from the battles' dead still unburied on the Lake Michigan shoreline. Street repairs in the early 1980s unearthed a number of human bones. First suspected as the victims of a cholera epidemic in the 1840s, the remains were later dated to the early 1800s and, due to their location, believed to be the remains of victims from the massacre. Semitransparent figures wearing pioneer clothing and military uniforms were spotted in a field north of Sixteenth Street running wildly, screaming in fear and fleeing for their lives.

CONGRESS PLAZA HOTEL

Adam Seltzer of Haunted Chicago Tours recommends the Congress Hotel, "which was only about two blocks away from the opening of 66. I can document a LOT of deaths in there, and guards have been talking about ghosts for years."

Faded as a soured old showgirl, wrinkly, smeared and stale, the Congress enjoyed an illustrious past as a prize along Al Capone's "Thousand Mile Stare." A jewel within the "Emerald City," constructed in 1893, the Congress Plaza Hotel proudly featured cobbled streets, gaslights and horse-drawn carriages. Originally known as the Auditorium Annex, it was constructed by Louis Sullivan, the fair's chief architect in 1893 as part of the World's Columbian Exposition. The original conception was an annex with a façade designed to complement Louis Sullivan's Auditorium Building, which sat across the street, at the time housing a remarkable hotel, theater and office complex. Built by noted hotel developer R.H. Southgate, the north tower was designed by Clinton Warren, with Louis Sullivan and Dankmar Adler as consultants. A much-celebrated feature of the hotel was an underground marble passageway called "Peacock Alley" that connected the new annex with the Auditorium Hotel, blending the two separate structures into one huge complex. In 1908, the name of the hotel was changed from the Auditorium Hotel to the Congress Hotel.

Built over the site of a skating rink, the Congress is marked as a place ripe for hauntings: a mysterious murder took place in the '20s, room 666 is sealed shut without explanation and unexplained noises coming from the hotel ballroom at night greet security guards but have no source as the ballroom is empty and quiet. Hallways are described as like in *The Shining*, complete with ghosts and typical poltergeist activity. Appliances turning themselves off and on are a mainstay of stories. In 1908, the hotel owners changed its name to the Hotel Congress, and it was known as the "Hotel of Presidents" housing Presidents Grover Cleveland, William McKinley, Teddy Roosevelt, William Howard Taft, Woodrow Wilson, Warren Harding, Calvin Coolidge and Franklin Roosevelt, while they met with their political constituency concerning campaign tactics at the hotel. It served as the Democratic locus for Franklin Roosevelt's presidential reelection in 1932.

The south tower was designed by renowned architectural firm Holabird and Roche, constructed between 1902 and 1907, and featured the Gold Room. The Florentine Room, a former roller-skating rink, was added to the north tower in 1909. These two rooms, along with the Elizabethan Room and the Pompeian Room, played host to Chicago's elite social events of the day. Benny Goodman, "The King of Swing," performed at the Congress Hotel from 1935 to 1936. After the Elizabethan Room converted to the Joseph Urban Room, an upscale nightclub complete with revolving bandstand, it became the headquarters for an NBC radio program.

Rumors claim that Al Capone frequented the Gold Room, used the hotel for his headquarters and even owned it. He is perhaps the most notorious ghost said to roam the halls (though if he stayed at the Congress, he must have used an alias for no records show he was there). The Gold Room was the first air-conditioned ballroom in the city of Chicago. During the 1930s, a man was shot in the ballroom, the victim of a love triangle. A mother committed suicide on the twelfth floor of the hotel by jumping from the balcony after tossing her three boys over the side; one of the children is now rumored to stroll through the Gold Room.

Ghost sightings include a six- to seven-year-old boy who walks around the ballroom at night, a piano that plays where no piano exists and what sounds like a fully active kitchen behind a curtained area off the ballroom. A lone man roams the eighth floor; the elevator, where a freak accident occurred, stops without being called; and voices are heard in empty rooms. Room 141, a room that security guards hate entering, is home to a shadow woman. A security guard entered Room 141 to take photos of the place at night, when he heard footsteps and saw the curtains opening and closing as if fingers were moving them. The twelfth floor also holds a room so frightening that the door was barred shut from the outside.

A workman is said to have been buried behind the walls during construction, and his gloved hand is seen sticking out of a wall in the closets behind the balcony of the Gold Room. Another ghost, "Peg Leg Johnny," was murdered inside the hotel years ago and haunts the location. Bridesmaids in wedding party photos taken within the Gold Room do not show up in the portraits if they stand near the piano. The fourteen-story property conceals other mysteries—like a hidden, sealed-off fifteenth floor—and secret escape routes might still exist.

Site of H.H. Holmes's Murder Castle

Jack the Ripper may have actually lived in America. H.H. Holmes is the first documented U.S. serial killer in the nineteenth century and has earned the moniker "Beast of Chicago." He was born Herman Webster Mudgett in 1861 (some accounts say 1860) in New Hampshire and changed his name as a young man. Among the aliases used in his lifetime were H.M. Howard, Herman Mudgett, Dr. Henry H. Holmes, Henry H. Holmes, Henry Holmes and H.H. Holmes.

He used the name H.H. Holmes when he attended medical school at Ann Arbor, Michigan, where he used his father-in-law's inheritance money for tuition. On July 8, 1878, Holmes married Clara A. Lovering of Alton, New Hampshire. Intelligent and unruly, he killed animals for sport. He was a cheat, swindler and fraud artist; in medical school, he took out insurance policies on cadavers and mangled the corpses to look like they were accident victims. He was nearly caught and left medical school, abandoning his wife and newborn child. No one knows where or what he did during the next five years before eventually turning up in Wilmette, Illinois, in 1885 posing as an inventor. Failing to divorce his wife, he remarried illegally to Myrta Z. Belknap in Minneapolis, Minnesota, on January 28, 1887. They had a daughter named Lucy Theodate. Holmes attempted to use his new father-in-law by forging his name on property deeds. He then moved to Chicago, where he began a copier business.

When the copier business failed, he worked in the Edgewood section of town at a drugstore on Sixty-third and Wallace Street for a Mrs. Dr. Holden. Druggists in 1887 were chemists, and most drugstores were stocked with elixirs and potions of all natures. Dr. H.H. Holmes compounded even the simplest prescription with a flourish, as an alchemist in the midst of some arcane ritual might do. He was a handsome, charming gentleman of fashion, wit and manners whose politeness and humorous remarks brought in new customers—most notably, the ladies. He spent more time working with the ledgers and soon acted as manager of the store and less as the prescription clerk, becoming the perfect assistant to the proprietress.

Mrs. Holden mysteriously disappeared in 1887 and reportedly bequeathed her store to him (or Holmes bought it, according to some accounts) just prior to her "moving out West," conveniently leaving no forwarding address. In 1890, he hired Ned Connor of Davenport, Iowa, as a watchmaker and jeweler. Connor arrived with his wife, Julia, and their daughter, Pearl. The family moved into a small apartment above the store. Julia was a six-foot-tall, green-eyed beauty with reddish-brown hair piled in curls on her head—just the type of woman to capture the interest of Holmes, who fired his bookkeeper and hired Julia to take the man's place. Connor began to suspect that Holmes was carrying on an affair with his wife and decided to cut his losses. Abandoning his family, Connor went to work for another shop downtown.

Once Holmes had Julia to himself, he took out large insurance policies on her and Pearl, naming himself as a beneficiary. Julia was suspected to be a willing participant in many of Holmes's schemes and swindles; she was listed, along with Kate Durkee, as director of the jewelry store after Holmes incorporated the business in August 1890.

Unsatisfied with the lot on which the store stood, Holmes purchased the lot across the street in 1889 and built his sixty-room hotel in 1892, with his accomplice Patrick Quinlan, to attract visitors attending the opening of the 1893 World's Fair in Chicago. The hotel occupied a full city block and housed nearly one hundred rooms, with many bizarre features: staircases that led nowhere, blind passageways, hinged walls, false partitions, rooms with no doors and rooms with many doors, doors opening to nothing, rooms without windows, trapdoors and hidden passageways, all centered on the second floor and all built from the mind of its architect: Holmes.

He had a reputation for hiring and then firing his construction crews in a fury, usually without payment. It is unclear if he paid for any of the materials used to build what would be later nicknamed the "Murder Castle" after the discoveries of Holmes's murders committed on-site (he confessed to twenty-seven). The first floor of the building contained stores and shops, the upper floors could be used as spacious living quarters and Holmes had an office on the second floor. The bottom floor had been used by Holmes as a drugstore, a candy store, a restaurant and a jewelry store. The third floor of the building had been divided into small apartments and guest rooms and apparently had never been used.

Julia was highly jealous of the female customers and would often sneak down the back staircase to spy on Holmes as he wooed his customers. Holmes installed a buzzer on the third step to alert him of Julia's approach; this system was repeated throughout the hotel. Julia's eighteen-year-old sister, Gertie, came to visit her in Chicago. Gertie was beautiful and quickly caught the eye of Holmes, who showered the young woman with gifts and affection, even telling her he would divorce his wife to be with her. Appalled at his behavior, Gertie left and went home, a move that saved her life. Julia, however, was deeply in love with Holmes, became pregnant with his child and sought marriage. Holmes insisted he would marry her only if she aborted the pregnancy.

In 1893, Holmes met a young woman named Minnie Wiliams, who became another mistress and, according to some accounts, another illegal wife. Holmes continued to push Julia into an abortion, assuring her he could perform the procedure. Holmes put Pearl to bed and brought the hysterical Julia down to his makeshift operating theater in his basement. Neither Julia nor Pearl was ever seen alive again, and one set of bones discovered in the basement was believed to have been Pearl's.

During Holmes's confession, he admitted that Julia had died during a bungled abortion he performed on her. Plus, he admitted that he poisoned Pearl. He murdered them because of Julia's jealous feelings toward Minnie Williams. "But I would have gotten rid of her anyway," Holmes said. "I was tired of her." Minnie Williams lived at the castle for over a year and knew more about Holmes's crimes than any other person. Holmes later confessed to killing Minnie, too, although her body was never found. It's thought she joined other victims in the acid vat in the basement.

Iron plates blocked the guest room windows, the rooms' doors locked from the outside only and guest rooms had their drapes drawn constantly. Hidden behind Holmes's apartments were various rooms; newspaper sketches of that time from the *Baltimore Sun*, *Chicago Tribune* and others carrying Holmes's tale of horror listed the "five-door room," "secret room," "mysterious closed room" (behind which was a dummy elevator for lowering bodies into the basement), "black closet," "room of the three corpses," "sealed and bricked room," "blind room" and the "hanging chamber," numbering nearly forty rooms total in this area.

Rooms were sealed shut and utilized as gas asphyxiation chambers, while others had been lined with iron plates and had blowtorches mounted into the walls to burn his victims. Other people were electrocuted or disposed of via acid vats or lime pits that could dissolve a body in a matter of hours. Much of H.H. Holmes's torturing was allegedly done on the second floor. Its design was a maddening maze of rooms and doors and a clandestine vault that was only big enough for a person to stand in. Investigators realized the implications of the iron-plated chamber after finding a single scuff mark of a footprint on the inside of the door the size of a woman's shoe, indicating someone had kicked the door in attempts to escape the locked vault. The second level also held thirty-five guest rooms, in addition to the odd assortment of rooms used for torture. Half of these were fitted as ordinary sleeping chambers with indications of occupation by the women who worked for Holmes, by tenants during the fair or by the unlucky women Holmes seduced before killing them. Several of the rooms had no windows and could be made airtight by closing the doors.

The subterranean basement was located seven feet below the rest of the building and extended out under the sidewalk in front of the dwelling. It was like something from a modern horror movie. Investigators found a surgical table in a room spattered with blood, gleaming surgical instruments, a crematorium, Holmes's macabre "laboratory" of torture devices, various jars of poison and even a wooden box that contained a number of female skeletons. In a hole in the middle of the floor, more bones were found. After being examined by a physician, they were believed to be the bones of two children between the ages of six and eight. Chutes from the prison rooms slid bodies directly to the basement. A total of 50 missing persons were eventually traced to Holmes's castle by police, though likely there may have been somewhere close to 250 victims who may have found their end in the Murder Castle. Because of the high count of bodies at the Murder Castle on the south side, it was rumored that there was a second drop location in a glass-bending factory on the north side. The location was torn down in the 1900s, and the area once covered by the hotel is a parking lot. Rumors of lights flashing on and off are associated with the area.

After the World's Fair, Holmes left Chicago, murdering people as he crossed the country. On January 17, 1894, he married his third wife, Georgiana Yoke, with Minnie Williams as a witness. He juggled all three wives, each unaware of the others. After his marriage to Georgiana, Holmes purchased several railroad cars of horses using counterfeit banknotes with the signature "O.C. Pratt." The horses were then shipped to St. Louis and sold. In July 1894, Holmes was arrested for the first time in Boston as he was preparing to leave the country by steamship—not for murder but for one of his horse-swindling schemes. Under the personae H.M. Howard, Holmes awaited bail from Georgiana and befriended a Mr. Marion Hedgepath, who was arrested for an insurance fraud scheme similar to what Holmes had done in medical school. Holmes developed a new plan: fake Hedgepath's death and collect the insurance money. Holmes had already partnered with Benjamin Pitezel to collect $10,000 from a life insurance company using the same plot. The insurance company suspected fraud and refused to pay. Holmes killed Pitezel to collect the insurance money and then convinced Pitezel's widow that her husband was still alive. Concerned that the five Pitezel children might expose him, he went away with three of the children, eventually killing them. After Holmes refused to pay him for his part in the scheme, Hedgepath went to the authorities

H.H. Holmes.

reporting Holmes, which then prompted an investigation and led to the grisly find at Holmes's hotel.

In his own defense, Dr. Holmes said, "In conclusion, I wish to say that I am but a very ordinary man…and to have planned and executed the stupendous amount of wrongdoing that has been attributed to me would have been wholly beyond my power."

The castle mysteriously burned down between Holmes's arrest and his planned execution. Three explosions were heard by neighbors, and the castle was gone. Rumors range from an accomplice trying to hide his implication to an outraged neighbor who wanted the curious thrill seekers to stop coming by the location. The case was notorious in its time and received wide publicity via a series of articles in William Randolph Hearst's newspapers. Holmes was executed via hanging at Moyamensing Prison in Philadelphia on May 7, 1896.

CHAPTER 3

JOLIET

Joliet was founded in 1831 by settlers attracted by well-timbered, gently rolling prairies; abundant acres of fertile soil; and soft coal and limestone deposits. Following the Black Hawk War, Charles Reed built a cabin along the west side of the Des Plaines River. Across the river in 1834, James B. Campbell, treasurer of the canal commissioners, laid out the village of Juliet, a name coined by local settlers. In 1845, local residents changed the community's name from "Juliet" to "Joliet." The city was officially established in June 1852 and prospered as a principal transportation corridor for both river and railroad traffic. The "City of Steel" emerged with the construction of the Joliet steel mill in 1869, and Bessemer converters installed in the 1870s were some of the earliest used in the United States. Limestone with bluish white tinges, quarried here, also earned Joliet the nickname "City of Stone." With the Chicago Fire of 1871 spurring demands for stone by 1890, Joliet was shipping over three thousand railroad carloads of stone a month to Chicago and other cities.

Joliet holds its own in frequency of paranormal events, including numerous sightings of ghost cars, footsteps and strange noises at the old Joliet Arsenal ammunition plant and EVPs at the Joliet Iron Works.

Potter's Field Cemetery (also known as the County Farm Cemetery) on the grounds of the old Will County Poor Farm contains forty-eight stones with no names, only numbers, except for one with the name George Miller. It is believed there are another 150 people buried here. Human remains have been located, and sightings included numerous reports of cold spots and ghost lights.

Hiram B. Scutt Mansion

The mansion is a west-facing, three-story, red brick, Second Empire/Italianate–style structure built circa 1882. On a Joliet limestone foundation and designed by architect James Weese, the mansion looms over Broadway. Hiram Scutt was a prominent Joliet businessman. He was president of Citizens Electric Company, part of General Sherman's army that captured Atlanta and held ten patents for varieties of barbed-wire fencing. He started the Joliet Barbed Wire Company and was the president of the Joliet Wire Check Power Company.

His beautiful home was nicknamed "Barb Villa" after his patented wire. Dominated by a three-and-a-half-story protruding tower (rumored to be a lookout post for Hiram Scutt to keep an eye over his barbed-wire factory), the home is capped with a Second Empire mansard roof and distinctive, bracketed tin cornice. It was the first house in Will County to have electricity and air conditioning. At one time, the home was a residence for young women called the Hannah Harwood Girls' Home.

Hiram lived in the home he built for a mere seven years before he fell from a horse in 1889 and died. This, however, was not the first tragedy in the home. Hiram and Addie, his wife, had two children, Frank W. and Grace, both of whom died in infancy. The house was later sold to Daniel Robertson, who allowed a variety of women's schools, such as the Business Woman's Club House, to operate in the mansion. He lived in the mansion until 1916. The longest continuous use of the home was from about 1916 to about 1977, when it became the home for professional young ladies, after which it again became solely a single-family residence. Recently, the house has been opened to the public as a banquet hall. It was listed on the National Register of Historic Places on February 5, 2003.

Hotspots of activity include Seth's Room and the library on the second floor and the Doll Room on the third floor, where cold spots are experienced. There have been some untimely deaths on the property, with one in the front yard as recently as 2006. Two murders are tied to this mansion, as well as at least two deaths of past owners. Entities seen include a woman dressed in dark clothing and a ghostly mob of people who walk through the street in front of the mansion.

Rialto Square Theater

The "Jewel of Joliet," the historic Rialto Square Theatre, reflected Italian Renaissance, Greek, Roman, Byzantine, Rococo, Venetian and Baroque architecture. At a cost of nearly $2 million to build, it opened on May 24, 1926. The theater played host to hundreds of patrons and a couple resident ghosts. A lovely spectral woman is sighted at the theater, possibly a former actress. She's young and surrounded by hazy lights. She appears floating to staff, customers and workmen and is most active during hours the theater would have been closed to the public. "My name is not Rachel; it's Raquel," she's reported to have told one woman.

Two other spirits, a male and female, are seen in the auditorium balcony, and their legend is that they fell to their deaths from the balcony. Another woman roams the hallways.

Opening-night theatergoers paid fifty cents to see the silent movie *Mademoiselle Modiste*. The *Joliet Herald News* described the theater before its grand opening: "When the doors of the new Rialto open tomorrow, Joliet will have one of the finest theaters in the United States, as experts say there is nothing to compare with it in any city of similar size, and it stands on even terms with the modern motion picture palaces of Chicago and New York."

The "Palace for the People" hosted Andy Williams, Mitzi Gaynor, Red Skelton, Victor Borge, Liberace and hundreds of others and was one of Al Capone's favorite haunts. One of the top ten theaters in the country and on the National Register of Historic Places, it is home to the Rialto School of the Arts.

Colin (though some accounts name him "Kevin"), a young spectral prankster, may have been hit by a car outside the Rialto in the 1930s and died inside the theater. However, there's no confirmation that any child died at the Rialto. This spirit received his name from a band crew member (the first person to see him) and doesn't like being called by the wrong name. He (with a telltale laugh) and the spirit known as the "White Bride" are most often seen walking along the promenade that looks down on the Joliet theater's rotunda. They (captured on film by TV's *Ghost Hunters* in an episode titled "Curtain Call") join the sightings of a man from the Prohibition days and a woman who is seen sitting at the organ. Among the ghostly activities and experiences here: lights turn on by themselves; a shadow figure is seen at a door leading to the auditorium; seats flip into a down position on their own; doors open and close; people are touched; clothes are tugged; icy cold spots are experienced; black masses are seen; moans, voices and unexplained noises are heard in the green room; the refrigerator door opens by itself; people are "jabbed" by an unseen bony finger; and objects move on their own.

FRANK SHAVER ALLEN HOUSE

Frank Shaver "F.S." Allen (1860–1934) was a significant Joliet, Illinois–based architect who achieved national recognition for his work. The haunting of his house was well documented in the local press when a team of psychics and a Joliet newspaperwoman investigated the home. The family then living there had experienced supernatural occurrences for over a decade. Built for wealthy Allen in the latter half of the nineteenth century at the corner of Morgan Street and Dewey Avenue, it became the center of local media frenzy over poltergeist activity taking place there during the 1970s.

Allen is most known for designing public school buildings in the Richardsonian Romanesque style. Allen was also an Egyptologist. While working in Joliet, he designed Sioux City Central High School, Lincoln School (in Racine, Wisconsin) and the original San Diego High School. He designed three of Joliet's schools: Joliet Central High, Sheridan Elementary and Broadway. Frank left Joliet in 1904 and moved to Pasadena, where he died in 1930, but his architecture career rather abruptly ends around 1910. F.S. Allen was a founder of the Tournament of Roses Parade and acted as grand marshal circa 1906. Several stories tell of a nanny, a child, disembodied voices and an elderly woman who died from a terminal illness in the house, all joining Frank and other unidentified spirits as the resident ghosts. A boy received repeated visits from the nanny and was invited by the ghost child to join him forever as his playmate. Illusionary fires raged through the home without damage, doors slammed, odd odors were reported, shadow figures were seen and unexplained and eerie screams and voices rang throughout the house in a wave of supernatural occurrences. The activity appears to have decreased in recent decades.

Old Joliet Prison

The Joliet Correctional Center (Old Joliet Prison Park) operated from 1858 to 2002 and is featured in numerous movies and television shows such as *Weeds*; *Stir of Echoes*; *Joliet Prison*; *1914*, a silent film; *Red Heat*; *Derailed*; *Let's Go to Jail*; *Bones*; *My Fair Brady*; *Breakout Kings*; *The Untouchables*; and *The Blues Brothers*, where it serves as the prison from which Jake Blues is released at the beginning of the movie. Today, it's a free public park located just outside the Collins Street Prison, where tourists are welcomed to the creepy nature of the location by colorful signage proclaiming, "Get Locked Up...At the Old Joliet Prison" or "Visit Joliet: Stay for Ten to Twenty," encouraging people to have their photos taken outside the prison where part of the movie *Natural Born Killers* was shot. Locals have said it was the scary place your parents frightened you with.

In 1818, preparing for admittance to the Union, the inhabitants of the Illinois Territory wrote a constitution and elected both a governor and a legislature. Article VIII, paragraph 14, of the constitution incorporated concepts of reformation through punishment that was promoted in the East: "All penalties shall be proportioned to the nature of the offense, the true design of all punishments being to reform, not to exterminate mankind." Until then, punishments for criminal offenses consisted of public hangings; internment in rough, crude jails or the pillory; and floggings. The new reforms, rooted in Christian doctrine, continued the European workhouse philosophy, in which evildoers worked out the wages of sin

Medieval-style Old Joliet replaced Alton Prison (opened 1833, closed 1860) and was built utilizing convict labor at a total cost of $75,000. With space for 761 inmates, the Joliet-Lemont limestone buildings, complete with turrets and crenelated walls in the administration building, were designed by William W. Boyington (responsible for the Chicago Water Tower and the capitol in Springfield). Old Joliet was the state's first prison and is one of the oldest in the nation; its design was the model for all United States prisons. The first 33 inmates arrived in May 1858, and criminals and prisoners of war were incarcerated there during the Civil War. Even without running water, the prison was better than being in Chicago's notoriously cruel and unsanitary Camp Douglas. After the Civil War, there was a competition for work between the prison chain gangs and returning soldiers. Businessmen could rent prison convicts for work. By 1872, the population had reached 1,239, a record number for a single prison. In 1898, there were thirty-two deaths in a total prison population of 1,257; twenty-one of these were due to tuberculosis. The prison was tough and broke the spirits of bad guys like Frank Rande. He was a gunfighter and deadly shot who had killed a dozen men by the time he arrived in Joliet to serve a life sentence during the 1870s. At five foot six and weighing 140 pounds, the little convict quickly established himself as one of the meanest men in prison. During his last fight, he blamed a guard for his latest confinement in a solitary cell. He knocked down the guard with a heavy poker in the prison harness shop. Another convict pulled him off or he would have killed the guard. He was a "furious demon," as a newspaper article described. For that last fight, Rande was sentenced to spend the rest of his life in solitary. But after a week of silence, he hanged himself with his shirt tied to the cell door.

The headline in the *Joliet Daily News* simply said: "Kicks the Bucket." The story under it said the people of Joliet could now congratulate themselves over the end of the murderous career of the wretch. Like Rande, many tough convicts spent the rest of their lives inside Joliet's limestone walls and were then buried in the prison cemetery called Monkey Hill.

In 1879, the *Chicago Daily Tribune* ran a series of articles concerning a man named Toby Allen. In a letter sent to his Chicago alderman during his incarceration in the Joliet State Penitentiary, Allen alleged that the State of Illinois hired a witch to torment him. In the letter, Allen declared that the State of Illinois contracted a man named Johnson to practice witchcraft on the inmates; however, Mr. Johnson also allegedly brought about the deaths of several inmates. Johnson whispered in Toby's ear, compelling him to cut off one of his own fingers so that he couldn't work. An appeal to his alderman to have the mayor look into the matter and alleviate Allen's torment was sent, but no formal public action was ever taken.

Joliet housed famous inmates from celebrated cases, such as what was then deemed the "Trial of the Century": the trial of chilling child murderers Leopold and Loeb. Serial killer John Wayne Gacy (convicted of thirty-three murders) called a Joliet cell home before he was executed by lethal injection in 1994 at Statesville Correctional Center.

A front view of the prison was described as quite imposing. The core of the building is the warden's house, offices, guard hall, commissioners' rooms, dining rooms and officers' sleeping rooms occupying four stories, with the fifth or top story being utilized as a women's prison. Across the street, an annex, originally constructed around the turn of the century to serve as a women's prison, held a row of very small cells with tiny barred doors about waist high in the basement. This was isolation or "seg" (segregation) for the female prisoners who misbehaved. Rumors of these women being victims of regular abuse by the guards of the era add to the "bad vibe" of the location.

On each side of the warden's house were great cell-house wings, each three hundred feet long. This extended the prison frontage toward the south one thousand feet. Nine hundred fireproof cells of stone and iron, arranged on corridors with fifty on a tier, made up the bulk of the cell houses, with a capacity of 1,800 convicts. Each block of cells stood at the center of the cell house with a twenty-five-foot passageway clear around. Each cell was eight feet deep, four and a half feet wide and seven feet high and held two men. A double iron bunk was provided, with husk mattresses, straw pillows, sheets and heavy woolen blankets.

According to August Maue in his 1928 *History of Will County*, prisoners lived in "healthful, sanitary rooms" that were "cheerful, wholesome, and not coldly institutional." He noted that the Joliet prisoner "has such privacy and accommodations as to be protected against the physical and moral foulness of an adjoining criminal" in a condition that "although sanitary, is far from luxurious, and in which he can retain his self-respect."

On Saturday, June 19, 1915, Warden Allen and his wife, Odette, made preparations for a short trip to the hot springs in Indiana. Odette's dress was not finished from the dressmaker, and Odette decided to wait until morning.

Vintage postcard.

She encouraged Edmund to travel without her. Just after six o'clock the next morning, a fire broke out on the second floor of the warden's house. Guards and a few convicts from the volunteer fire department broke down the door to Odette's bedroom to extinguish the flames and found her dead. The coroner's report showed that her skull had been fractured by the water bottle found next to the bed. Once knocked unconscious from the blow, she became a victim of the smoke and flames that had been started by a container of alcohol and engulfed her bed.

"Chicken Joe" Campbell, a trustee who had been appointed by Edmund a few months earlier as Odette's personal servant, was charged and convicted on circumstantial evidence and sentenced to death. His sentence was later commuted to life imprisonment by Governor Dunne.

Riots, executions, dread, insecurity and a very real sense of mortal vulnerability that only those who have worked in such an institution can truly relate to added to tales of the murder of a warden's wife. Rumors of a singing ghost in the prison cemetery drew thousands of curiosity seekers in 1932. Residents on the hill above the old prison in Joliet first heard the eerie voice singing when the full moon moved across the sky on the hot night of July 16, 1932. Three thousand people gathered after reports of a ghost ran in a local paper, according to a book by Robert Sterling, yet no singer was heard. Officials later determined the singing had come from a musical night watchman who had a penchant for crooning to himself to stave off the lonely quietude of his post. Perhaps the prison isn't haunted by a singing ghost, but the singing was heard while the man deemed responsible was said to be digging a trench at the time, and one wonders how his voice was able to carry the distance to where the singing was heard.

The corner of Hermitage and Diversey Parkway was once the site of Adolph "The Sausage King" Luetgert's factory and the site of a murder. Luetgert killed his wife in the basement of the factory, where her remains were discovered. She haunted him during his incarceration in the Joliet prison until the day he died. On May 1, the anniversary of Louisa's death, she can be seen roaming her old stomping grounds.

In addition to Louisa's ghost and the mystery of the singing ghost, people report capturing images in the windows and feelings of unease and distress within the walls; a tug on a sleeve or goose bumps during a heat wave give rise to the possibility of a haunting on-site. Other ghostly activity has been noted at an old pauper's ground on the property that became Monkey Hill. The state did require the use of vaults in the cemetery, and if a fresh grave was dug too close to an existing one, the contents of the first grave could seep into the new one. Rumors of ghosts float around both the Joliet prison (Monkey Hill) cemetery and the Statesville prison cemetery, drawing the attention of paranormal teams and thrill seekers. Any inmate who died in the old Joliet prison and was unclaimed (meaning the state was responsible for the burial) would be in the Joliet prison cemetery. Unfortunately, no records exist for this cemetery. The markers were simple wooden crosses, the last of which decayed many years ago. Dozens of convicts had been buried in this cemetery during the 1800s.

"I don't think I'm guilty," said the stout, thirty-year-old George Chase. Authorities weren't sure that was his real name, and he wouldn't tell them. With blue eyes, sandy hair and whiskers, the *Joliet Signal* also described Chase as having a dead expression but still called him a "rather fine looking man." He was hanged anyway, the first execution in Joliet in the summer of 1866. Chase was convicted as a horse thief during the period of the Civil War and served time in the prison on Collins Street. In the spring of 1864, he attempted to escape, hitting Deputy Warden Joseph Clark in the head with a club. Clark died a few weeks later, and Chase was charged with murder. In January, Chase was sentenced to death on the gallows, but it wasn't until a year and a half later that he faced the noose. On July 27, 1866, a Friday, Chase was led from his jail cell at around 2:30 p.m. to a gallows made of two posts on each side of the hallway with a beam over the top of them. The hangman's noose dangled from the beam, with the opposite end extending through a hole into the basement. At the end of the rope were tied three heavy sandbags down in the basement, serving as a spring. Chase was followed by three ministers reading from Bibles, his only visitors during his months of imprisonment, and they stayed with him through the final hours.

"I don't see any proof that I murdered that man. I think I've got as good an explanation of that as you have," he said. As a white hood was draped over his head, Chase was reported to say, "I'm not ready for that yet. I'm as innocent a man as any of you. I am as innocent a man as any in the United States. I admit that hanging is justice. But hanging for a thing a man ain't guilty of and can't prove I am guilty of is another thing. It ain't justice." He complained that the ropes on his arms and legs were too tight, and then uttered his final words, "Gentlemen, I am to be slaughtered."

The *Joliet Signal* account read, "When the spring was touched, he was launched into eternity."

"He was thrown up some five feet and hung with his feet about 3½ feet off the floor," the *Joliet Republican* reported. "He died with scarce a struggle."

His body hung in the jail hallway for about twenty minutes before being taken to a funeral home, where his head was removed and his brain examined by doctors hoping to find a clue to criminal behavior. However, the *Joliet Signal* said, "The brain was sound, showing no signs of insanity."

Chase's head was given to the phrenologist for use in his lectures, and the headless corpse was buried in the prison cemetery.

CHAPTER 4

WATSEKA

Taking a tour ninety miles south of Chicago, just a jaunt off Route 66 and one hour and twenty-nine minutes southeast from Joliet is the town of Watseka, named for the wife of settler Gurdon Saltonstall Hubbard. Hubbard, born on August 22, 1802, was a friend to the Indians and an adopted son of Chief Waba of the Kickapoo. The Indians called Hubbard "Pa-pa-ma-ta-be," translated as "Swift Walker," after he walked seventy-five miles in a single day to bring settlers in Danville to Chicago to help fight off an Indian raid. When a local Indian tribe questioned this amazing feat, Hubbard challenged their champion walker to a race, who lost the race to Hubbard by several miles and was unable to move the next day. Hubbard appeared unaffected by the endeavor. Watseka or Watchekee was a Potawatomi Native American woman and niece of Chief Tamin of the Kankakees. She was born in Illinois around 1810 and named for the heroine of a Potawatomi legend. In 1826, she married Gurdon, and about two years later, they mutually dissolved the union.

THE "WATSEKA WONDER"

That is my daughter…Why, she has been in heaven twelve years. Yes, let her come, we'll be glad to have her come.
—*A.B. Roff*

In the town of Watseka, a large brick home with Gothic windows and a wraparound porch bore the reputation of being haunted. There were

Vintage postcard.

rumors of an entire family murdered in the basement, with the bodies buried beneath oak trees in the backyard, and tales of the demonic spirit possession of a young girl who was tormented until she hanged herself. However, the true tale of the house built in 1860 has brought even more attention to the still-standing home of the Roff family.

Mary Roff (October 8, 1846–July 5, 1865), daughter of a founder of the small town, began experiencing epileptic fits or possibly developed schizophrenia. During these fits, she spoke in different voices and told stories involving people miles away. Mary had a mania for bleeding herself with leeches; she went so far as to lovingly name the creatures. She died mysteriously at age eighteen (some accounts say nineteen) in the Peoria, Illinois insane asylum after a harrowing and ghastly descent into madness in which she slashed her arm with a razor. Her lifetime of violent fits and seizures robbed her of her youth, personality and, finally, her soul. Many assumed she was mentally ill, but some believed that her illness was something beyond natural. Her family was soon convinced their daughter had been possessed by the devil, becoming, as Dr. E. Winchester Stevens wrote in his account of the incident, "a raving maniac of the most violent kind." Mary often entered a clairvoyant state, with no normal sense of sight or sound, and didn't recognize anyone, even family members. If blindfolded, she could see and read books without the cover being open. She was placed in the sanatorium after her parents, Asa and Ana, found her on the floor, bleeding, with a razor still in her hand. They regretted their decision forever.

Modern-day researchers suggest that individuals with seizure disorders or temporal lobe disturbances are often associated with poltergeist activity and other psychic traits. Mary complained of creatures or people following her and became convinced that her blood was poisoned. The girl had attempted suicide once before her father finally gave up and, taking drastic measures, placed her in the mental institution.

In 1877, things were different, and many of these cases were easily dismissed as insanity. Early American society referred to individuals suffering from mental illnesses as "lunatics," derived from the root word "lunar," meaning "moon." Popular belief held that insanity was brought on by a full moon at the time of a baby's birth or a baby sleeping under the light of a full moon. Colonists declared lunatics possessed by the devil, removing them from society and keeping them locked away. Causes were many and varied and included: intemperance in drink, religious excitement, fright and nervous shock, love affairs (including seduction), old age, a wife going against her husband's wishes, a female's critical (menstrual) period and education. Doctors of the day believed the onset of insanity came from an illness, lack of sleep or poor nutrition. Dr. Benjamin Rush, a preeminent physician during Abraham Lincoln's time, stated that observable symptoms of insanity included: "a wild and ferocious countenance; enlarged and rolling eyes; constant singing, whistling and hallowing; imitations of the voices of different animals; walking with a quick step, or standing still with hands and eyes elevated towards the heavens—the madman, or maniac, is in a rage."

"Cures" for mental illness amounted to what we would now consider a form of torture. Mary was treated to the "water cure" that harkened back to the Middle Ages. She was immersed naked in a tub of icy water and then dunked into scalding hot water. Female inmates were given icy douches via a hose, and water-soaked sheets were tightly wrapped around them to calm them, squeezing the blood vessels with vasoconstriction.

In an 1843 report to the Massachusetts legislature seeking social reform for the treatment of the mentally ill and prisoners, Dorothea Dix, a leading advocate for these patients, said, "If I inflict pain upon you, and move you to horror, it is to acquaint you with the sufferings which you have the power to alleviate (cure), and to make you hasten to the relief of the victims of legalized barbarity."

America's first documented possession in 1877 concerned thirteen-year-old Mary Lurancy Vennum (called Lurancy, or Rancy), who was possessed by the spirit of Mary Roff. A bizarre case encompassing not one but two families unfolded, causing many to believe the spirits of the dead were alive and communicating messages to the living, even temporarily inhabiting another body. An article appearing in the September 1879 issue of the *Religio-Philosophical Journal*, titled "The Case of Lurancy Vennum," written by Dr. E. Winchester Stevens, stated, "Her insanity, as it was thought to be, dates from July 11th, A.D., 1877, and the remarkable phenomena continued until her perfect restoration through the aid of friendly Spiritualists and spirits on the 21st of May, 1878."

Mary Lurancy "Rancy" Vennum was born on April 16, 1864, and on July 11, 1877, she told her mother she wasn't feeling well. Five hours later, she went into a cataleptic fit and was unconscious for five hours. Upon awakening, she told her family she felt "very strange and queer," but she slept peacefully that night. According to Stevens's account:

The next day the rigid state returned, and passing beyond the rigidity, her mind took cognizance of two states of being at the same time. Lying as if dead, she spoke freely, telling the family what persons and spirits she could see, describing them and calling some of them by name. Among those mentioned were her (deceased) sister and brother, for she exclaimed, "Oh, mother! Can't you see little Laura and Bertie? They are so beautiful! There

*were people in my room last night and they kept calling 'Rancy! Rancy!'
and I could feel their breath on my face."*

The Watseka Wonder, an 1879 booklet by Dr. E.W. Stevens, can be found in
the public domain and was written by the spiritualist doctor who witnessed
the one-hundred-day, continued spirit control of young Lurancy Vennum
and wrote about the case.

Christopher Saint Booth and Philip Adrian Booth produced a documentary
on the Lurancy case called *The Possessed*, in which they said, "The belief
in possession by evil spirits plagued the eighteenth century. Madness and
hysteria spread, classifying the mentally ill as being under the control of the
Devil. These sad misfits became the victims of bizarre exorcisms or casting
out rituals. Banished from society, they were locked away inside brutal
asylums. Some called them angels, others called them devils, and they all
were branded *The Possessed*!" Lurancy's experience is described as "a chilling
journal of a thirteen-year-old girl from the small town of Watseka, Illinois,
who became possessed by spirits of the insane dead!" The Booth brothers'
documentary was originally part of the prior *Children of the Grave* film, but so
much information was obtained that it morphed into a project of its own.

I questioned Philip Booth about their movie project and whether they
experienced any activity while on the sites filming. His answer via our
written messages was: "Quite a few, would you like me send you a copy they
are documented in it, (the movie) if you have the chance watch the making
of for the general case background."

Then there is Dr. E.W. Stevens's account of what happened in November:

*On Nov. 27, 1877, she was attacked with a most violent pain in her
stomach, some five or six times a day; for two weeks she had the most
excruciating pains. In these painful paroxysms, she would double herself
back until her head and feet actually touched. At the end of the two weeks,
or about December 11, in these distressed attacks, she became unconscious
and passed into a quiet trance, and, as at former times, would describe
heaven and spirits, often calling them angels. Once out of her trances, the
girl couldn't remember anything that she said or did.*

*Beside themselves, her family was ready to have the girl committed after
the family's Methodist minister and two physicians declared her insane.
Incarceration in an asylum was recommended. It was said that Lurancy's
behavior mirrored that of "Methodists at a revival."*

From public domain work of Dr. E. Winchester Stevens.

Snake-handling was often part of a Methodist tent revival, as explained in the article "Religious Revivals and Revivalism in 1830s New England" from teachushistory.org:

> *The well-organized Methodists had many types of religious meetings on a regular basis. A practice which particularly scandalized the orthodox was the active participation of women in quasi-leadership positions. Although they sometimes went so far as to preach before a mixed audience, or spoke in tongues, they more often witnessed, testified, exhorted, or led female prayer groups.*
>
> *After a while, exhortation alternated with the singing, eliciting congregational ejaculations of "Amen!", "Glory!", or "Jesus!" As the penitent came forward to the anxious seats, exhortations and singing became simultaneous. Ministers and others also entered this altar area, encouraging the anxious to pray and give their hearts to Christ. Many were "slain," that is, swooned under the power of the Spirit; some danced and shouted; some cried.*

Watseka's newspaper published the girl's tale and reported her strange jabbering. Townspeople claimed Lurancy was a medium, able to communicate with the dead, and said that she spoke in strange voices, sharing involved stories. Asa Roff, hearing of the events at the Vennum home, vowed to keep another girl from dying at the hands of "ignorant and bigoted strangers" and called Dr. Stevens of Janesville, Wisconsin, to examine the girl. When Asa visited the Vennum family on January 31, 1878, Lurancy was found sitting by the stove, "very sullen and crabbed," calling her father "Old Black Dick" and her mother "Old Granny."

Doctors were convinced that Stevens (a spiritualist) had hypnotized Lurancy into believing she was Mary. Stevens and the Methodist minister spent time alone with her, leading some to wonder what influence they might have had over her behavior. Lurancy would have known of the Methodists' behavior during tent revivals, and in a small town such as Watseka, she could have heard the grim tale of Mary Roff, even though the account states the families did not know each other. (Another source indicates that the Roffs' contact with the Vennums was a formal speaking acquaintance between the two men and a phone call that was never returned.)

Keep in mind that the American spiritualism that took hold of the United States in the decade before the Civil War into the early years of the twentieth century was very much alive and well in Illinois during this time. The Roffs became avid Spiritualists after Mary's death.

During Stevens's interview with Rancy, she sat unblinking, her legs drawn up tight beneath her, hands clasped before her, her countenance resembling a mean, grouchy old woman. In a manner not to be trifled with, she claimed she was Katrina Hogan, age sixty-three, from Germany. Her voice was raspy, and she growled that she didn't want to be disturbed.

When asked how long she'd been there, Lurancy (as Katrina) replied, "Three days." Stevens then asked, "How did you come?" to which Katrina responded, "Though the air." When Stevens asked, "How long can you stay?" Katrina responded, "Three weeks."

Suddenly, she changed personalities, saying she was lying and now was a young man named Willie Canning who lived a wild life and possibly committed suicide. Willie said he was present "because I want to be here."

An hour and a half later, Lurancy fell on the floor in a trance and spoke "with rationality and understanding," saying her "evil conditions" were influenced by evil spirits—Willie and Katrina. Stevens suggested that Lurancy find a higher being as her guide, and the girl announced one was there by the name of Mary Roff (Lurancy was one year old at the time of Mary's death). With some amount of discussion with other spirits, Lurancy said she was going to allow Mary to take possession of her body.

At that time, Stevens documented, "From the wild, angry, ungovernable girl, to be kept only by lock and key, or the more-distressing watch-care of almost frantic parents, or the rigid corpse-like cataleptic, as believed, the girl has now become mild, docile, polite, and timid, knowing none of the [Vennum] family but constantly pleading to go home." During the period Mary occupied Lurancy's body, she (Mary) stated that "Lurancy was away, being treated, and would come back when she was restored to health, both mentally and physically. When Lurancy was ready to return, 'Mary' must leave."

Lurancy recognized Minerva Alter, Mary's older sister, as her sister Nervie (a pet name given by Mary and unused since the young woman's death) and Ana as her mother. Lurancy (as Mary) wanted to go home to the Roffs, and on February 11, 1878, the Vennums allowed it. When asked how long she would stay, the reply was: "The angels will let me stay until sometime in May." She lived with the Roffs until May 21, not eating for the first month of her stay, saying her nourishment came from heaven. She recognized both neighbors and other family members and recalled events that Mary participated in with her family. Asa tested Lurancy with a velvet hat Mary wore before her death, to which Lurancy declared, "Oh, there is the headdress I wore when my hair was short."

Lurancy did not know anything of her own true life during this time, and one day while in a trance, another spirit with ties to Tennessee came through, saying Mary would occupy the girl's body until it was restored to health. The Roffs also held séances in their front parlor. On April 21, 1878, Mr. and Mrs. Roff; their hired woman, Charlotte; Dr. Steel and his wife; Dr. Stevens; and other friends gathered to witness peculiar manifestations. Dr. Steel was taken over by the deceased brother of one of those attending the séance and spoke to the room. Once disentranced, Mary left Lurancy's body, which fell over like a corpse. Mary immediately took control of Dr. Steel. She laughed at Lurancy slumped lifeless on the shoulder of her neighbor and then abruptly left Dr. Steel, returning to Lurancy.

The minister who tried to have Lurancy committed told Mrs. Vennum, "I think you will see the time when you will wish you had sent her to the asylum."

Lurancy told of the time Mary cut herself with a knife. She began to raise her sleeve to show the scar but halted and said, "This is not the arm; that one is in the ground." She described how it felt, who saw it done and where the arm was buried as well as a message she'd written to her father via a medium with the name, time and place. Another instance was a rapping session and spelling conducted through another medium. The Roffs admitted the truth to Lurancy's story. Lurancy also displayed clairvoyance as Mary warned of her "brother's" impending illness.

On May 7, the girl called Ana into a private room to announce that the real Lurancy was coming back. A change of personality then took place, and Lurancy began crying, wanting to go home, but after about five minutes, Mary returned. Mary was finally ready to leave Lurancy on May 21 at 11:00 a.m., saying the young girl was in good health, and Mary was ready to go to heaven.

Later in life, when Lurancy was married and in labor, Mary once again inhabited her, resulting in a painless childbirth.

Ghostly occurrences are associated with the Roff home. Door handles rattle; EVPs include sounds of violence and possible sexual abuse, references from when the building was a brothel; white figures are seen, as well as faces in the walls; psychics report a tall man, a woman and two younger girls, as well as shadow figures. There are cold spots, feelings of becoming ill, choking sensations, whispers in the house, a voice replying "the devil" to questions asking identity, objects and furniture moving, loud bangs, unexplained touching, voices, growls and fragrances of flowers. The basement has had several incidents of individuals being scratched, and recordings capture lights and a phantom train whistle. There is a belief that a portal has been opened due to the use of a Ouija board on the premises, and some believe Mary haunts the home.

To this day, the case draws interest, and some believe the "Watseka Wonder" was an early, undocumented case of multiple personality disorder. It is also believed that upon reaching puberty and going through the time of life where most poltergeist-type activity is alleged to occur with girls of that age, young Lurancy sought attention as a catalyst and gathered enough details that she was able to create an entirely separate personality, extracting more information later from the family.

Cover of Dr. E. Winchester Stevens's book about the possession of Lurancy.

Mary's grave is in the Watseka GAR cemetery. Urban legend says it is always warm to the touch, no matter the weather or temperature. Members of the Vennum family are buried here as well, except for Lurancy, who is buried in Kansas.

PONTIAC

The fourth generation of his family to live there, Jesse W. Fell was born on November 10, 1808 (died 1887) to Jesse and Rebecca Roman Fell in New Garden Township, Chester County, Pennsylvania. Jesse's great-grandfather had arrived from England in 1705. The third of nine children in a Quaker family, he was admitted to the Illinois bar in Jacksonville in 1832 and traveled through Springfield, where John Todd Stuart recommended homesteading in the new town of Bloomington. Fell passed through New Salem, Pekin and Delevan on his way to Bloomington; founded (some accounts say co-founded) the towns of Clinton, Towanda, Lexington, LeRoy and El Paso; helped develop Dwight, Joliet and Decatur; established a post office in Pontiac; and founded Illinois State University. A close friend of Abraham Lincoln, Jesse urged him to challenge his opponent, Stephen A. Douglas, to their famous series of debates. Fell named the town of Pontiac after the legendary Ottawa Indian chief who became famous for his role in Pontiac's Rebellion (1763–66), an American Indian struggle against the British military occupation of the Great Lakes region following the British victory in the French and Indian War. Fell had a strong economic presence and important friends among railroad officials. His influence ensured that the railroad passed through Pontiac (with the station located in Fell's First Addition) and bypassed Richmond, two miles east. Fell was the great-grandfather of the governor of Illinois, Adlai Stevenson.

Southside Cemetery in Pontiac has a local folk tale of a memorial chair that produces the sound of a woman's scream if you sit on it during the dark of night and rub its arms, all the while reciting the words inscribed on its back.

HUMISTON WOODS

Humiston Woods is an Indian burial site where there are still remains of Indians, many of them children's bones. When children play around this area, they tend to feel a pull at their legs as if someone is trying to use them to get out or someone is trying to pull them in. It's thought that the spirits of Indian children buried in the woods are trying to get some attention or perhaps get out of the ground. The *Atchison Kansas Globe* of February 2, 1882, wrote, "A ghost for the past two weeks has been doing business in the woods near Pontiac, Illinois. He is white above the waist and dark below and flames appear from his mouth and nose." The article went on to say the ghost came out of a log cabin and sent a group of ten children into a frightened stampede. An expedition led by a correspondent of the *Chicago Times* investigated but did not find the ghost.

Indian mounds in Cahokia. *Courtesy Janice Tremeear.*

CHAPTER 5

BLOOMINGTON

Bloomington's downtown sat at the edge of a large grove frequented by the Kickapoo before Euro-American settlers arrived in the early 1820s to create the settlement of "Blooming Grove" in 1822. They kept the designation of a village until 1831, when the population grew to 150, and the first jail was built in 1832. Abraham Lincoln rode the circuit to Bloomington to conduct business in the Miller-Davis building. A disastrous fire around the turn of the century consumed a huge portion of downtown, north and east of the courthouse. The burnt area was rebuilt by local architects George Miller, Paul Moratz and A.L. Pillsbury. Route 66 was built along the Chicago and Alton Railroad corridor, bringing business and tourists into a town where Dorothy Louise Gage died in 1898 at five months old. The niece of Maud (Gage) Baum and L. Frank Baum, the author of *The Wizard of Oz*, the character Dorothy is said to be inspired by the child and named after her. Maud was the original name for the main character, but Baum's wife was so distraught over the death of her niece that Baum named the character of Dorothy in honor of the infant. Ghosts said to wander the town include the last Illinois democratic presidential candidate, a lost little girl and murderous millionaires. Ghosts are not the only oddities known to the residents of Bloomington; the UFO Casebook website and the UFO reporting groups MUFON (Mutual UFO Network) and NUFORC (National UFO Reporting Center) have all recorded cases of flying objects over the city. Thunderbirds were spotted in 1977 in Pekin, Bloomington,

Tremont and rural Mclean County on telephone poles and trees. A land-bound creature described as a large black panther was sighted around Bloomington. The odd 1942 case of human combustion in downtown Bloomington occurred when janitor Aura Troyer burst into flames in the basement of the bank, with no known cause for the fire. In the spring of 1970, northeast of Bloomington, the Farmer City "Monster" was sighted and reported as a "a bigfoot monster" very much resembling the "Kickapoo Monster" sightings that also occurred during the 1970s.

In the winter of 2009, a truck driver and his wife were driving along Interstate 47 heading south when the full-bodied apparition of a Native American rose from the earth in a vision seen by the wife. The man stood in a harvested cornfield and had a powerful, charismatic bearing. He wore a small feathered headpiece of white buckskin with a beaded design in blue and red. He stood with his arms to the sky and communicated the injustices done that drenched the fields in the blood of his people, stating that they must not be forgotten, nor their suffering be in vain. He is believed to have been Kennekuk (Kanakuk), the Kickapoo Prophet.

PHOENIX MID-CITY HOTEL

Built around 1902, this European-style hotel flourished until 1965, when business died off and the building was vacated. The hotel lay dormant as time took its toll on the twenty-six upstairs rooms and objects within the hotel. Inside, one could find newspaper clippings and front pages scattered everywhere across the floor and children's toys in a chest, untouched for decades. It's said a man died of a heart attack in one of the rooms, and now his ghost grabs people by the leg to get attention. Piano music is heard playing throughout the building, cold breezes occur on hot days, shadow figures are seen and a child's voice has been captured on recordings.

ILLINOIS WESLEYAN UNIVERSITY

Illinois Wesleyan University came into being through a long list of lawyers, doctors, teachers, tradesmen, mechanics, farmers and ministers seeking to create "an institution of learning of collegiate grade." The United Methodist

Church supported the university, lending "Wesleyan" to the original name of Illinois University. Situated on eighty tree-filled acres, the central portion of the present campus was acquired in 1854. The oldest building is Stevenson Hall, built in 1910, and bears the motto *Scientia et sapientia*, or "Knowledge and wisdom," coined by famed explorer and Wesleyan professor John Wesley Powell. Old North Hall, the first building, was erected in 1856. After 110 years, it was removed in 1966 and replaced by Sheean Library. "Old Main"—Hedding Hall—was built in 1870 and destroyed by fire in 1943. Post–World War II development gained momentum, and most of the buildings were constructed after this time.

International House—a Classical-revivalist mansion that featured imported woods, servants' quarters, ballroom on the third floor and a library—was finished in 1907 as the residence of A.E. DeMange and his wife, who were Bloomington's most prosperous citizens. After only one year of living in the house, Mrs. DeMange died of natural causes, leaving her widowed husband alone and grief-stricken. He abandoned the house but left it fully furnished for three years before selling it to the university in 1911. It was then established as a women's dormitory. This building is said to be haunted. The porthole window at the service stairs of the mansion turned residence hall shows the reflection of the ghostly image of the house's former mistress; candle in hand, she's said to follow people up the stairs. A resident assistant interviewed in the *Bloomington Pantagraph* in 1993 said, "You feel something follow you up the stairs, and you can see something from the corner of your eye reflected in the glass, but if you turn around and face it, you won't see anything." The ghost sightings show up in resident scrapbooks dating back to 1979: "In the master bedroom stands a full length mirror, which has remained there for 80 years. She appears again before the mirror, dressed in her favorite red dress, preparing herself for the elaborate ball, her reflection is clear in the moonlight shining on the mirror."

A 1981 article stated that a lovers' quarrel at the ball in 1880 led to the spirit choosing to remain in the ballroom, where she dances alone—through the walls. It's said there was an old elevator in the building in which a young man was trapped and died when it fell. Though it has long been sealed up, the squeals of gears and snapping cables are still heard, along with the crash of the elevator smashing onto the basement floor.

The young niece of the university president roams the third floor after dying in the building; her laughter can be heard throughout the floor.

The house of music fraternity Phi Mu Alpha is alive with supernatural folklore. A doctor and his family had the home built in 1898 in Franklin Park, and the legend surrounding the house can bring nightmares to the squeamish. The physician's daughter is said to have fallen in love with a young sailor in town. She became pregnant, and to prevent a scandal, her father attempted to abort the child. The procedure failed and caused the girl's death. The horrified father was now mentally unstable and, in his unhinged state, dismembered her body. He carried her remains to the dumbwaiter and lowered them into the basement, where he then buried her in the floor. The spirit of the girl roams the building after her tragic end, and the bricks marking her grave are rumored to sink into the ground even with continuous replacements. The girl's tale surfaced in the mid- to late 1960s, along with a description of her wearing a heavy white veil as if dressed for a wedding. She's also been described as a "humanoid ethereal form" sitting on a couch. Regardless of her form, her visitations were never threatening. A type of burial service was held for her in an attempt to put her at rest. The location of the "grave" was blessed and a whitewashed cross painted on a door nearby. It's said that as long as the cross remains, the house will be protected.

Adams Hall was built in 1965 and is the home of the Acacia fraternity. Legend states that three women, all named Frances, haunt the house. Frances #1 was struck by a carriage, carried into the house and died within. Franceses #2 and #3, a young girl and an older woman, also perished in the house, from unclear causes. Sounds of a rocking chair emanate from the unoccupied room above, and lights have been found on in the unoccupied rooms on the upper floor. In August 1970, a resident experienced several phone calls assumed to be pranks, but all phones were removed from their hooks, and still the ringing continued. Stereos have been turned off and on in unoccupied rooms, cold blasts of air come from the guest bathroom and footsteps are heard on the stairs.

CHAPTER 6

SPRINGFIELD

S pringfield has a long-standing reputation as being haunted. Lincoln has been seen walking the streets surrounding Springfield's original courthouse and the hallways of his former home. Mary Lincoln is seen at their old home, located at 413 South Eighth Street. The ghostly encounters include: apparitions of a woman, toys moving of their own accord and the unique event in April on the anniversary of Lincoln's death, when two phantom funeral trains draped in black and adorned with black streamers ride the same tracks that bore his body to Springfield in 1865. Mournful music pours from the first train. The second tows a flatcar with Lincoln's coffin. The procession never reaches its final destination.

Springfield's original name was Calhoun, after Senator John C. Calhoun of South Carolina. The future site was still unbroken prairie when Illinois entered the Union in 1818; Elisha Kelly first explored the region coming from North Carolina in 1819. The city became the state capital in 1837, and railroads arrived in 1852. The Donner party began their ill-fated journey at Springfield. A large race riot erupted in 1908 that resulted in the lynching of two African American men and the deaths of four whites killed by the defenders of the black area of the city. Rumors of the city being the safe point for those who took part in Chicago's St. Valentine's Day Massacre were a subject of debate among the residents, and hints of a bootlegging connection linger. One of the haunted locations of the city is the Prairie Capital Convention Center, where a boy was killed at a tractor pull and now doors slam

Left: Donner Party plaque.

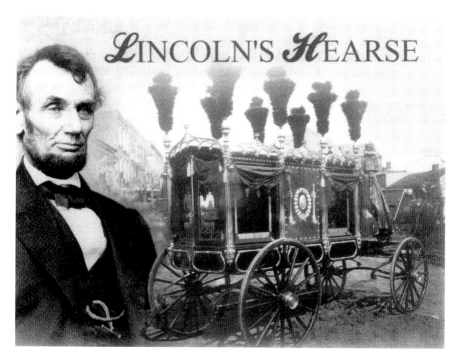

shut as the child wanders about at night. An actor named Joe was mugged and murdered in a back alley after a performance here and haunts the location.

VIRGIL HICKOX HOUSE

Built on land purchased from Paschal P. Enos in 1839, Springfield's oldest and last single-family residence still stands in the downtown business district frequented by the elite. Virgil Hickox lived in the house from 1839 to his death in 1880. He was a store owner; prominent attorney; railroad developer, responsible for bringing the Chicago and Alton Railroad to the city; canal commissioner for the Illinois and Michigan Canal; bank president; and chairman of the Democratic State Committee for twenty years. Allied with Stephen Douglas, he was personally and professionally linked to Abraham Lincoln.

Springfield's first men's club, the Sangamo Club, occupied the house after Virgil's death in 1895. Illinois governors were given honorary membership in the club, which operated for fifteen years. Once the Sangamo Club vacated, it converted to Branson's Funeral Parlor, with a casket room on the lower level. During the 1918 Spanish influenza epidemic, Branson's operated twenty-four hours a day, flooded with victims of the deadly flu.

During Prohibition, a speakeasy operated in the lower levels. Hoot Francis was given one of the first liquor licenses in the city to operate a tavern on-site. Norb Anderson reopened the place in 1937 as Norb Andy's Tabarin, bringing in nationally known celebrities like Tommy Dorsey. Phantom footsteps, voices, doors opening and closing, objects moving and pictures falling off the wall have been reported. People are touched, a male figure (thought to be Norb) with crossed arms peeks out of a window and a young girl named Alice shares space where many believe a portal to another world exists.

DANA THOMAS HOUSE

The "Jewel of Springfield" was Frank Lloyd Wright's first "blank check" commission. Started in 1902 for one of Springfield's leading citizens, Mrs.

Susan Lawrence Dana, who lived in the house from 1904 until about 1928, it became a symbol of culture and high society in the city. She and her family are said to haunt the house, along with a dark spirit. The unexplainable events coincide with Dana's birthday, the day her mother died and the days that three funerals were held in the home. Susan's family thrived following the Civil War, investing heavily in the expanding rail service. Their Italianate villa was a prominent feature in town, and when Susan married Edwin Ward Dana in 1883, her father, R.D. Lawrence, was a very wealthy man. The newlyweds moved to Minneapolis, where Edwin's business failed, forcing them to Chicago, where Edwin's new company failed after a year. In disgrace, he borrowed money from Lawrence and moved back to Springfield. Sent to manage a mine in Oregon, he soon was on the move again when it closed. In Leland, Oregon, this time, he left Susan at Grants Pass; however, within a month, she returned to Springfield with Edwin's body. He was crushed while hoisting ore when a harness snapped and the pulley arm spun in reverse, striking him in the chest and killing him. Not only had Susan lost her husband but also two infants she was unable to carry to term.

On February 17, 1901, R.D. Lawrence died in his Springfield home, giving Susan financial freedom and another tragic blow. She decided to build a grand new home for the family, including her mother, her grandmother (who would pass away in August 1902) and her cousin, Flora Lawrence. She found young designer Frank Lloyd Wright, who was just starting in Chicago, and he was intrigued by her ideas. The old villa would incorporate a new addition. Wright planned a Prairie-style house, long and horizontally shaped with open spaces inside, with furniture and windows that do not obstruct the interior. Staircases were all hidden, interior walls were all cream-colored and crossed with fabulous woodwork, and the library had built-in bookcases with glass fronts. Beneath the walkway to the gallery were a billiards room and a bowling alley.

Susan became enamored with Spiritualism, believers of which included some of the most respected and influential people of the 1800s and early 1900s, such as Sir Arthur Conan Doyle, Sir William Barrett, Elizabeth Barrett Browning, James Fenimore Cooper, Washington Irving, Henry Longfellow and James Greenleaf Whittier. She soon hosted parties for the holidays of 1904.

She held regular séances with the elite of local society. In March 1912, Susan secretly married a concert singer from Denmark named Jorgen Constantin Dahl, fueling the gossip mill since her new husband was half her age. One year later, he died. In 1915, she married again to Charles Gehrmann of Springfield, but she and Charles divorced in 1930.

Susan Lawrence Dana Dahl Gehrmann lived however she pleased. An advocate of women's rights, she actively participated in the suffrage movement and was named as the Illinois chairman for the National Women's Party in 1923 working for women's rights to vote. She collected many books on the occult, and her Spiritualist group called itself the Springfield Society of Applied Psychology and, later, the Lawrence Metaphysical Center.

Money finally ran out, forcing her to close down the grand house. Flora was gravely ill, and the two of them moved into the Lawrence cottage, located across the railroad tracks from the house. Flora died in 1928, and Susan was in poor health. She consulted mediums, as she had always done, and, prompted by spirits, changed her name to Susan Z. Lawrence. She kept in touch with Frank Lloyd Wright over the years, but their last meeting was canceled when Susan fell down the steps of the cottage and was injured. She entered St. John's Hospital in May 1942 and would never leave. A court petition declared Susan incompetent and unable to handle her affairs, and Earl Bice, a court-appointed attorney, served as conservator of the estate. Farnetta Radcliffe, a Chicago cousin, was Susan's caretaker. Susan had kept all of her father's properties intact, including the Springfield buildings, the house and abandoned mines in Colorado and Oregon. An auction was held in July 1943 to dispose of her goods to cover her debts; Charles C. Thomas, book publisher, purchased the house.

Susan passed away on February 20, 1946, lucid and aware of her surroundings. Her home holds the phantoms of Susan's life: sad humming coming from the billiards room in a downstairs portion of the home; sounds of folding chairs being thrown down the stairs, footsteps and clapping hands; light sconces flying off the walls; coatroom doorway curtains floating back and forth; and a woman dressed in black who walks downstairs from the master bedroom down a second flight to the basement. During the summer, the outdoor balcony becomes deathly cold, even in the Illinois heat.

INN AT 835

Built in the early 1900s, first as luxury apartments, the inn was the dream of Bell Miller, a turn-of-the-century businesswoman. It was designed during the Arts and Crafts movement by architect George Helmle. Her dream home was completed in December 1909 with exquisite oak detailing, airy verandas and massive fireplaces. In a neighborhood once termed "Aristocracy Hill," the dignified building attracted an array of blue-blooded tenants.

But Bell became so enamored of her dream home that she refuses to leave. A ghostly figure has been seen drifting through doorways, a warm and friendly voice is heard and a book from a tightly packed shelf has been found placed in the middle of the room on multiple occasions. When wallpaper began peeling away from the wall, it was perfectly repaired by the next morning. Sounds of the lid from a crystal candy dish being removed and replaced are heard, and guests report that, regardless of the button they push in the elevator, they wind up on a different floor.

LINCOLN HOME

It is portentous, and a thing of state;
that here at midnight in our little town;
a mourning figure walks, and will not rest;
near the old courthouse pacing up and down…
—*Vachel Lindsay, "Abraham Lincoln Walks at Midnight"*

Abraham Lincoln had bizarre dreams and visions and was always melancholy due to the death of his mother when he was still a child. This, along with hard labor to make an existence in the wilderness and his struggle for an education, made him a serious man, even when he was making a joke.

Lincoln's most famous vision while living in Springfield came during the 1860 presidential elections. He returned home in the early morning hours amid news of victory after nightlong celebrations in his honor. Going to his bedroom, he collapsed onto a settee. Nearby was a large bureau with a mirror, and Lincoln's reflection in the glass was a prophetic vision. His face was two images, with the tip of one nose three inches from the other. The second time he saw it, one face was clearer and much paler than the other, holding the coloring of death. He told his wife, Mary, of the strange vision and attempted to conjure it up again in the days that followed. The faces always returned to him, and while Mary never saw it, she believed her husband when he said he did. She also believed that she knew the significance of the vision. The healthy face was her husband's "real" face and indicated that he would serve his first term as president. The pale, ghostly image of the second face, however, was a sign that he would be elected to a second term but would not live to see its conclusion.

Lincoln's first inauguration and ball on March 8, 1861, was called a "monster levée," and a "monster gathering." The ball, originally limited to two hours, continued for two more and was described by a terribly enthusiastic writer as "a jam, it was a rush, it was a cram, it was a crush, it was an omnium gatherum of all sorts of people, an 'irrepressible conflict,' a suffocating pressure, an overwhelming manifestation of private interest and public curiosity in the new dynasty without precedent for comparison in the history of this government."

The most crippling blow Lincoln suffered while in the White House was the death of his third son, William "Willie" Wallace in 1862; his second son, Edward "Eddie" Baker, had already died at three years and ten months old. Thomas "Tad," the youngest, only lived to age eighteen, leaving first-born Robert Todd as the only Lincoln child to see adulthood. A week after Willie's funeral, Lincoln locked himself away in his office and wept all day, and he may have been on the verge of suicide. Mary fell into an advanced state of depression. Lincoln became desperate to bring her out of her despair and took Mary to the window, pointing out a nearby asylum, and said, "Mother,

Lincoln Home.

LINCOLN'S PROPHETIC DREAM OF APRIL 1865

Three days before his assassination, Lincoln discussed the following dream with Ward Hill Lamon, Lincoln's friend and biographer:

About ten days ago, I retired very late. I had been up waiting for important dispatches from the front. I could not have been long in bed when I fell into a slumber, for I was weary. I soon began to dream. There seemed to be a death-like stillness about me. Then I heard subdued sobs, as if a number of people were weeping. I thought I left my bed and wandered downstairs. There the silence was broken by the same pitiful sobbing, but the mourners were invisible. I went from room to room; no living person was in sight, but the same mournful sounds of distress met me as I passed along. It was light in all the rooms; every object was familiar to me; but where were all the people who were grieving as if their hearts would break? I was puzzled and alarmed. What could be the meaning of all this? Determined to find the cause of a state of things so mysterious and so shocking, I kept on until I arrived at the East Room, which I entered. There I met with a sickening surprise. Before me was a catafalque, on which rested a corpse wrapped in funeral vestments. Around it were stationed soldiers who were acting as guards; and there was a throng of people, some gazing mournfully upon the corpse, whose face was covered, others weeping pitifully. "Who is dead in the White House?" I demanded of one of the soldiers. "The President," was his answer; "he was killed by an assassin!" Then came a loud burst of grief from the crowd, which awoke me from my dream. I slept no more that night; and although it was only a dream, I have been strangely annoyed by it ever since.

do you see that large white building on the hill yonder? Try and control your grief, or it will drive you mad, and we will have to send you there." Lincoln may have believed in the supernatural: he participated in séances held within the White House, and many guests were Spiritualists. Several gave him dire warnings about his future, and Lincoln adapted a fatalistic attitude, convinced he was doomed.

It's said that medium Nettie Maynard conducted a séance in 1863 and was playing the grand piano when it began rising from the floor. Lincoln and Colonel Simon Kase were both present and climbed onto the piano. It shook and jumped so hard that the men climbed down. Lincoln referred to the levitation as an "invisible power."

Criticism and rumors about Mary began almost immediately, exacerbating her emotional and physical problems (devastating headaches that kept her bedridden for days at a time). She may have fallen into the beginnings of her insanity after Willie's death and continually consulted mediums to communicate with her lost son. Her dreadful temper swung in manic extremes from gracious, charming hostess to angry, depressed virago. These emotional episodes were becoming more frequent and less easily hidden. In May 1875, Mary Todd Lincoln went to trial on the charge of insanity and was committed to an insane asylum by her son Robert, although she later won her release. On July 16, 1882, Mary Todd Lincoln died at the home of her sister in Springfield, a victim of paralysis. In no other couple in American history was the husband held in such glory yet the wife so vilified.

Lincoln purchased the Springfield home in 1844, still a small cottage with pine exterior boards, walnut interiors, oak flooring, wooden pegs and hand-made nails. It had three rooms on the first floor and sleeping lofts upstairs, and a bedroom expansion on the first floor later became the back parlor. The large kitchen was split into a formal dining room and kitchen. In 1850, Lincoln improved the exterior of the property by adding a brick wall and a fence along Jackson Street. Through 1855–56, the Lincolns added the second story, with three bedrooms and a master "his and hers" bedroom suite. Mary is thought to haunt the home: a woman is seen standing in the parlor who abruptly vanishes, rustles of crinoline dresses are heard, cold spots are experienced, voices and music played on the piano are heard and a key missing from a wooden chest in Mary's room turned up in the lock on the piano tied with a bit of pink ribbon. People feel their hair being brushed, and a woman is seen lurking about the house, tapping visitors on the shoulder. The most common sight is a rocking chair moving on its own.

Lincoln is thought to haunt the White House, the courthouse, his tomb and his former home in Springfield. He is a polite ghost, asking people to leave his bedroom by saying "please" and "thank you." He's seen on the steps carrying papers or hurrying down the stairs, never speaking, and he walks through people. An older white female is also seen in the living room with a cleaning rag in her hand.

Oak Ridge Cemetery

The oldest actual haunting connected to Abraham Lincoln concerns his tomb, where strange sobbing noises, ceaseless pacing, tapping footsteps on the tile floors, whispers, quiet voices and the sounds of someone weeping are heard.

Lincoln's body was returned to Springfield to a remote, wooded cemetery called Oak Ridge after his assassination in April 1865. Started around 1860, the cemetery consisted of woods and unbroken forest with iron gates and a caretaker's residence. Grave robbery and the posthumous wanderings of Lincoln's corpse may account for the cemetery's hauntings.

On April 15, 1865, the day after President Lincoln's assassination, a group of Springfield citizens formed the National Lincoln Monument Association to construct a memorial/tomb to receive the body of the president. On the morning of April 21, 1865, a train of dark-garlanded cars departed from Washington City with two bodies onboard: the late President Abraham Lincoln and his son William. The 1,654-mile funeral journey took thirteen days, during which the body was viewed by hundreds of thousands of people. The train dubbed "The Lincoln Special" traveled through 180 cities and seven states and made eleven stops along the way as it retraced the route Lincoln had taken to Washington for his first inauguration, allowing the public to pay their respects as he lay in state. Approximately three hundred people accompanied Lincoln's body on the journey, including his eldest son, Robert.

After the corpse arrived on May 3, Lincoln's body was prepared for burial by the undertaker and embalmer. The coffin was transported to an elegant hearse finished in gold, silver and crystal loaned to Springfield by the City of St. Louis. It lay in state in the capitol for a night. Following the funeral the next day, Lincoln was placed within an aboveground white marble sarcophagus in a tomb at Oak Ridge Cemetery, the site Mrs. Lincoln had requested for burial. In December 1865, the remains were removed to a temporary vault near a new proposed memorial site. In 1871, or three years after laborers had begun construction of the permanent tomb, the body of Lincoln and those of three of his sons were placed in crypts in the unfinished structure. Curiosity seekers said the spectral image of Lincoln himself roamed near the crypt, investigating the broken ground where his tomb would someday stand. In 1874, after completion of the memorial, Lincoln was interred in a marble sarcophagus in the center of a chamber known as the catacombs, or burial room. On November 7, 1876, several Chicago criminals broke into the tomb, intent on kidnapping the corpse for ransom. One of the men in the gang was a spy for the Secret Service, and the grave robbing failed. Lincoln's body was then hidden. On the night of November 15, 1876, John Carroll Power, tomb custodian, and a select group of trusted confidants elected to hide Lincoln's coffin in the basement of the tomb. They tried to dig a grave in the basement but found that water seeped in wherever they dug, so they simply set the coffin on the ground and covered it with bits of lumber left over from the tomb's construction, disguising the coffin as a woodpile. This was to be a temporary placement for the almost-hallowed remains, but there they remained until November 1878. They then removed the coffin to yet another unnamed location near the base of the obelisk and buried the coffin under a few inches of dirt. On February 12, 1880, the seventy-first anniversary of Lincoln's birth, these same men, joined with three others of the association, met and formed what was to become known as the Lincoln Guard of Honor.

In 1899, the tomb itself had become dangerously weakened by the shifting of the earth beneath, making a reconstruction necessary. The dismantling of the tomb began at once, and on March 10, 1900, the remains of all of the Lincoln family bodies were moved to a temporary subterranean vault built just for that purpose. On April 24, 1901, Lincoln's remains were viewed to ensure this was indeed the former president's body. State officials, members of the former Lincoln Guard of Honor, Robert Lincoln, a few invited guests and two police officers on duty, George Cashman and Robert Lindley and their sons, whom they smuggled into the tomb beneath their coats, were those on hand to view the remains. The lead-lined coffin was opened, the body with its chalky white skin and mildewed clothing was confirmed to be Lincoln's and the coffin was resealed for the last time. The workmen were called, and it was returned to the catacomb, where it was lowered into the prepared vault. Its estimated Lincoln's body has been moved seventeen times.

Along with the specter of Lincoln, the Oakridge Cemetery is haunted by the apparitions of a small boy and a mysterious woman in a flowing red cape.

CHAPTER 7

NEW SALEM

T he reconstructed village of New Salem, situated on a hill one hundred feet high overlooking the Sangamon River, began as the dream for a river town made prosperous by a hoped-for trade route. On July 19, 1828, John Cameron entered a tract of land along the Sangamon and applied to the state legislature for permission to build a dam across the river at a spot called Fish Trap Ford, which was near the only major road in the area. Cameron and James Rutledge, both shrewd businessmen, realized the significance of the site and located their mill at the crucial crossing on the main overland route. Plots for a town were sold, and by 1828, the population was abuzz with riverboat talk. On January 22, 1829, work began on a dam. Wooden bins were built in the river, with local farmers providing wagons and teams hauling nearly one thousand wagonloads of rock from nearby streams to fill them. A combination grist- and sawmill was constructed on a platform over the river, and the venture drew customers from miles around for a rough frontier settlement on the northern edge of civilization. In the glory days, it was not unusual to see forty horses tethered to the trees on the steep hillside, described by locals of that time as standing with "their heads forty-five degrees above their hams."

In April 1831, a flatboat hung up on the dam at the mill below the village, and the boat's crew fought to save the craft from sinking. Due to the quick thinking of one of the young men, most of the cargo was unloaded, and what remained was shifted to the stern of the boat. After wading ashore to borrow an auger from the town cooper, he bored a hole in the bow, draining

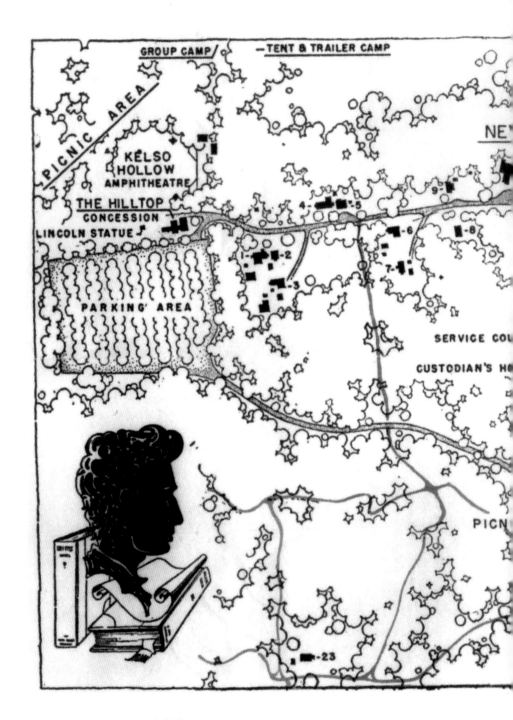

New Salem vintage souvenir folder.

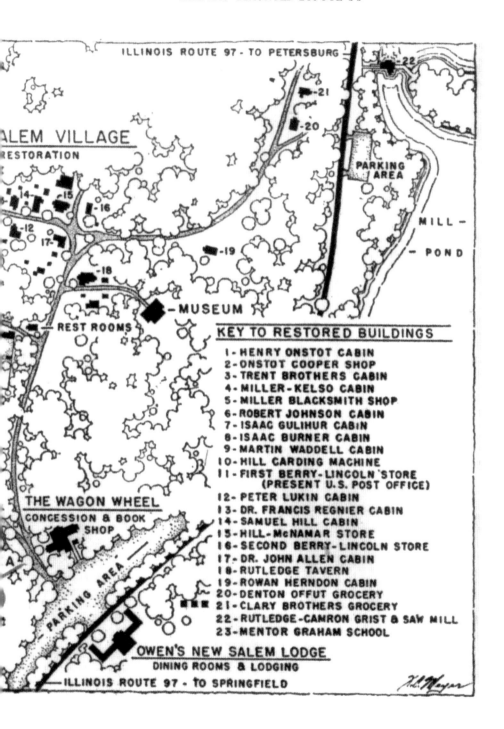

ILLINOIS ROUTE 97 - TO PETERSBURG

—22

—21

—20

PARKING AREA

SALEM VILLAGE
RESTORATION

MILL —

— POND

—14 —15

—16

—12

17—

—19

—18

—MUSEUM

— REST ROOMS

KEY TO RESTORED BUILDINGS

1- HENRY ONSTOT CABIN
2- ONSTOT COOPER SHOP
3- TRENT BROTHERS CABIN
4- MILLER-KELSO CABIN
5- MILLER BLACKSMITH SHOP
6- ROBERT JOHNSON CABIN
7- ISAAC GULIHUR CABIN
8- ISAAC BURNER CABIN
9- MARTIN WADDELL CABIN
10- HILL CARDING MACHINE
11- FIRST BERRY-LINCOLN STORE
        (PRESENT U.S. POST OFFICE)
12- PETER LUKIN CABIN
13- DR. FRANCIS REGNIER CABIN
14- SAMUEL HILL CABIN
15- HILL-McNAMAR STORE
16- SECOND BERRY-LINCOLN STORE
17- DR. JOHN ALLEN CABIN
18- RUTLEDGE TAVERN
19- ROWAN HERNDON CABIN
20- DENTON OFFUT GROCERY
21- CLARY BROTHERS GROCERY
22- RUTLEDGE-CAMRON GRIST & SAW MILL
23- MENTOR GRAHAM SCHOOL

THE WAGON WHEEL
CONCESSION & BOOK
SHOP

PARKING AREA

OWEN'S NEW SALEM LODGE
DINING ROOMS & LODGING
— ILLINOIS ROUTE 97 - TO SPRINGFIELD

the water, and then plugged the hole, whereby the boat slipped effortlessly over the dam. He was an ungainly youth dressed in a pair of blue jean trousers rolled up at the cuff; a cotton shirt, striped white and blue; and wearing a buckeye-chip hat for which a price of twelve and a half cents would have been exorbitant at the time, but he managed to salvage the situation. He returned in July 1831 to run a store for Denton Offutt, owner of the flatboat, and introduced himself to his new neighbors as Abraham Lincoln, giving rise to the mythological aspect of New Salem's origins. He stayed for six years before relocating to Springfield.

Don't ask the park guides if the village is haunted. They will deny it, yet tales persist, and one of the ghosts might be from a tragedy that happened there.

On January 18, 1833, Lincoln was helping to repair a broken bed at Rutledge Tavern and found he needed a certain tool to finish the job. Lincoln sent ten-year-old Nancy Rutledge to Rowan "Row" Herndon's to borrow a tool. Nancy described the sight that greeted her: "When I arrived there, Mr. Herndon was loading his gun to go hunting, and in getting ready to go out, his gun was accidentally discharged, and his wife, who was sitting near, talking to me, was shot right through the neck. I saw blood spurt out of each side of her neck, her hands flutter for a moment; then I flew out of the house and hurried home and told Annie and Mr. Lincoln what had happened." Elizabeth died instantly. Row moved away soon after, amid whispers that his wife's death was anything but accidental.

The *Sangamo Journal* of January 25, 1833, reported on the accident:

> *We learn that on Wednesday last, while Mr. R. Herndon of New Salem was preparing his rifle for a hunting excursion it went off, and the ball, striking his wife in the neck, separated one of the principal arteries, and in a few moments she was a corpse. It is hardly possible to conceive the anguish of the husband on this melancholy catastrophe. The community in which he lives deeply sympathize with him in this afflicting event.*

Elizabeth may still be in New Salem. Reports list a woman in a pure white dress or shrouded in white, and children see the woman in the pretty dress. The ghost of a woman is spied near the far end of the village, walking along for a few steps and disappearing, and sometimes she carries a broom. Weird things happen, and the form of a man wearing dark clothes and a tall hat, with his foot propped up in midair, accompany disembodied footsteps, cold spots and the feeling of being watched.

CHAPTER 8

CAHOKIA

Old Route 66 follows today's I-270 from the north side of St. Louis. Another noteworthy side trip to the east of the Gateway Arch, approximately fifteen minutes away, is one of Illinois' biggest attractions. Early history of East St. Louis is intertwined with the history of Cahokia, the village three miles south of the present city. Cahokia (meaning "Wild Geese"), named after a tribe of Illinois Indians, was settled on December 7, 1698, by missionaries from the Seminary of Quebec, led by Vicar General Francis Jolliet de Montigny. The vicar general assigned Father Saint Cosme to proselytize the Indian inhabitants of the village. Originally the summer camp of the Tamoroa and Cahokia tribes, one-fourth of the population elected to remain during the winter of 1698. By May 1699, Father Cosme had built a crude church. It was the first permanent European settlement in Illinois and became a center of French influence in the upper Mississippi River Valley. The Ottawa chief Pontiac was killed at Cahokia in 1769.

Constant flooding of the village drove the inhabitants to higher ground to establish a settlement they named Illinois City. Fifty-eight years later, Illinois City was absorbed by East St. Louis.

Philip François Renault, a French explorer and favorite courtier of King Louis XV, had been appointed director of mines in the French colonies in 1719. In that year, he set out from France for Illinois. A metallurgist, Renault believed there were precious metals to be found in Illinois. He sailed aboard a ship called the *Maria* with a company of some two hundred miners, technicians and laborers. At Santo Domingo,

Monks Mound information sign. *Courtesy Janice Tremeear.*

Renault bought five hundred slaves in 1720 and brought them to Fort de Chartres in Illinois, thus introducing slavery into the Illinois country. Witchcraft trials might have occurred at the Cahokia Courthouse. John Reynolds, fourth governor of Illinois and a resident of Cahokia, said, "Several poor African slaves were immolated at the shrine of ignorance for the imaginary offense" of witchcraft in Cahokia in the late 1700s. According to Reynolds, "The ancient French in Illinois believed that the Negroes in the West-India Islands possessed a supernatural power to do injury to anyone that incurred their displeasure, and had the power, also, to look into futurity. The power, the old French ladies believed, came from Africa." These superstitions originated from observations of slaves practicing voodoo.

The first instance of voodoo practiced in the French villages of Illinois occurred in a deposition made by Bernard Gibkin at St. Louis on December 29, 1778. Gibkin was a physician and ordered by Fernando de Leyba, governor of Spanish St. Louis, to examine a black slave belonging to Marie Laurent. Gibkin stated, "I perceived that the sickness by which he [the slave] was attacked proceeded from a violent poison. His body was in convulsions and his limbs rigid on account of the corrosive poison."

Before the slave died, he accused Baptise Bastein, a slave belonging to the Saucier family. Interrogated by the court at Cahokia concerning the murder, Baptise denied poisoning the other man but admitted to serving the dead man a glass of wine in his master's house. The court decided not to pass judgment in the case; however, six months later, the Cahokia court reopened the murder case. During the proceedings, a series of poisonings by other individuals with tinges of black magic was uncovered and involved two slaves from Cahokia: Manuel and Moreau.

Moreau was accused of poisoning the aforementioned slave of the Laurent family because of jealousy over a woman by the name of Janette. Janette was feared in the village of Cahokia, according to the book *History of St. Clair County, Illinois, With Illustrations and Biographical Sketches of Some of Its Prominent Men and Pioneers*. Grown adults and children were terrified by her approach, and many believed she held the power to destroy people and their property with her incantations.

On the basis of the evidence, Colonel John Todd, lieutenant commandant of the county of Illinois, condemned Moreau to be burned at the stake on the banks of the Mississippi. He later ordered a militia captain to guard Moreau from the mob and administer a merciful execution. Moreau was hanged and Manuel shot. No actions were taken against Janette. At their executions, it was reported that a flock of crows was seen flying over the scene believed to be the spirits of the two witches turned into birds and taking flight. True history concerning slaves executed in Cahokia for witchcraft may never be known, but it would be comparable to known examples of the fear of witches, racial prejudice and ignorance of the American frontier.

CAHOKIA MOUNDS

Built here by the indigenous Mississippian culture while Europe was in the Dark Ages, ancient Cahokia is the oldest town in the state of Illinois in the Cahokia group of mounds. Covering 4,000 acres (2,200 of which are preserved as a state historic site), it is the largest archaeological site in the United States, with 120 structures composing the vast city. The top of Monks Mound is the benchmark hub or preeminent surveying station, to which all outlying mounds relate back. With a footprint of 14 acres, this colossus is larger at its base than the Great Pyramid of Khufu at Giza. The two largest Indian mounds at this site are Monks Mound and the Rattlesnake (or Harding) Mound, which is located at exactly 380 degrees, 38 minutes, 38.8 seconds north of the equator. Archaeologists tell us Monks Mound was built between AD 900 and 1200 and named after Trappist monks who farmed the terraces in the early 1800s. It is a stepped pyramid that covers about sixteen acres and was rebuilt several times in the distant past. At the summit of the mound are the buried remains of a temple, further adding to the mystery. Don't expect the works of the pharaohs: symmetrical, grass-covered hills sitting in flat, lightly wooded bottomlands give way to the view of the Gateway Arch in distant St. Louis from the one-hundred-foot top of Monks Mound, lending an odd sense of grandeur.

Another vast set of mounds only seven miles away on high bluffs above the Mississippi River in what became Old St. Louis township, conspicuously within view from an observer's position atop Monks Mound of the Cahokia set, was far-off Big Mound, dominating the distant western skyline. Our image of what Indian life was like on this continent before Europeans arrived has been forever changed by the discovery of these mounds. This collection of agricultural communities reaching across the American Midwest and Southeast before AD 1000 and peaking around the thirteenth century was foreign to Europeans. Their first encounter of the mounds and the ten-story earthen colossus composed of more than twenty-two million cubic feet of soil led them to believe they had found the work of a foreign civilization: Phoenicians, Vikings or a lost tribe of Israel. Henry Brackenridge, a lawyer and amateur historian, came upon the site and its massive central mound while exploring the surrounding prairie in 1811. "I was struck with a degree of astonishment, not unlike that which is experienced in contemplating the Egyptian pyramids," he wrote. "What a stupendous pile of earth! To heap up such a mass must have required years, and the labors of thousands." Cahokia's domain, the vast floodplain named the American Bottom, stretches from St. Louis to a long line of bluffs three miles east of Cahokia and as far to the north and south as the eye can see.

One of only eight cultural World Heritage sites in the United States, Cahokia's second-largest mound was razed by horseradish farmers for landfill in 1931, and the site has been home to a gambling hall, housing subdivision, an airfield and a pornographic drive-in. Archaeologists excavating Mound 72 found the remains of fifty-three women, one very high status man and the decapitated remains of four men who may have been on the wrong side of some sort of authority in evidence of ritual human sacrifice. Excavations

Monks Mound, Cahokia. *Courtesy Janice Tremeear.*

through the mound indicated that it had been constructed as a series of smaller mounds that were then reshaped and covered over to give the mound its final form. Within these smaller mounds, a series of features were excavated, mainly burial pits and burial deposits. More than 250 skeletons were recovered in various states of preservation. This belied the common belief that American Indians lived in egalitarian communities, without the brutally maintained hierarchies defining many other civilizations. Cahokia may have been a "theater of power," a hegemonic empire sustained by force and perhaps connected to Mesoamerican civilizations such as the Maya or Toltec. The entire city seemed to spring to life almost overnight around 1050, a phenomenon now referred to as a "big bang."

Yet there are some who are quick to point out that many large-stature skeletons were exhumed from the mounds during the nineteenth century and gifted into the collection of the Smithsonian Institute, never to be seen or heard of again. These skeletons differed markedly from the physiology of the Asiatic-Indians, and where hair was still visible, it was often red or blond in coloration. Many other such North American mound sites report the seven- to eight-foot skeletal remains of those who lived there. For those seeking this path of thought, the mound building, district by district, becomes clear when the individual positions of each mound are analyzed by proper surveying. Each structure is a precisely placed survey marker, residing at a coded distance and angle from a central fulcrum or hub mound. Cahokia may have been a navigation school or ancient open-air university to explain how the ancient lunisolar (relating or attributed to the moon and the sun) Sabbatical Calendar worked, as well as how three major lunar cycles were monitored and calculated.

The ghost of Mound 31 lurks in the elevation seen on Google maps showing the shape of the mound, torn down in 1960 to build a store called Grandpa's. Mound 30 was torn down for the construction of a nightclub. An auction liquidation house now stands where Mound 31 once stood.

Forty-eight wooden posts make up a 410-foot-diameter circle "Woodhenge," and when aligning the central observation posts with specific perimeter posts at sunrise, the exact date of all four equinoxes can be determined. Natchez Indians of the Lower Mississippi Valley, known for being devout worshippers of the sun, may be the descendants of the Mound Builders. According to legend, a bearded and robed god visited the Mound Builders, inspiring them to love one another, live in harmony with the land and build the great earthen works. Later, they degenerated back to human sacrifice and warfare. It's believed about twenty thousand

Stockade wall of the Cahokia Mounds Historical site. *Courtesy Janice Tremeear.*

people once occupied Cahokia, living inside a wooden stockade surrounding various pyramids. People streamed in from surrounding areas, built houses and constructed the infrastructure of a new city with a grand plaza the size of forty-five football fields. Everything from sporting events to communal feasts to religious celebrations brought thousands.

Described by the French as being the "most civilized of the native tribes," it was later reported that in 1725, the death of a chieftain touched off a sacrificial orgy among the Natchez when several aides and two of the man's wives agreed to be strangled so they could escort him into the next world.

In August 1987, Monks Mound was the meeting place of more than one thousand people taking part in a worldwide "harmonic convergence," which was designed to bring peace to the planet. Many Native Americans and metaphysical groups believe Cahokia is a sacred place and a source of powerful psychic energy even today.

As part of an experiment with Joshua Shapiro and the Crystal Skull Explorers in October 2011, I used dowsing rods to help measure bands of energy emanating from the skulls he had in his collection. We began in Missouri and made a pilgrimage atop Monks Mound at the Cahokia Mounds Historic Site to charge the skulls with the ancient energy of the Mound Builders. Ghostly activity associated with the site includes balls of lights, as well as sounds and apparitions of Indians.

GHOSTS OF THE MOUND BUILDERS

Less than ten miles to the west, the ancient Indian mounds that gave St. Louis the nickname Mound City in the 1800s were almost completely leveled by the turn of the century. Today, only one, Sugar Loaf, survives. Big Mound and at least twenty-five others are gone, and only some photographs and a dogleg road named Mound Street remain. East St. Louis and St. Louis fought a lengthy, losing battle against development and neglect for the better part of a century, eventually seeing both sites—among the largest Mississippian communities and mostly still present in the first half of the nineteenth century—destroyed and paved over. The burial chambers described copper, ivory and conch shells and were sisters to Cahokia in that the location was on a high terrace next to the Mississippi River.

The French named Big Mound, the largest of the St. Louis mounds, *La Grange de Terre* ("the Barn of Earth"). It is known alternately as Peale's Mound

27. It was measured with a compass by Dr. Thomas Say and Titian Ramsey Peale at 319 feet long and 158 feet wide, with a height of 34 feet and with three terraced approaches facing the river. They also identified twenty-seven "tumuli" (including Big Mound) within the mound group, though two may not have been Indian mounds.

A rough square border was formed by the mounds around a central plaza, with a semi-circular area on the west side composed of three smaller mounds. The enclosed plaza was three hundred yards in length and two hundred in breadth. An amazing mound within this group was the "Falling Garden," nearly fifty feet high and rising in three stages up to the second terrace. Forty earthen structures were part of this landscape. Sixteen mounds were destroyed in Forest Park to prepare for the World's Fair in 1904.

Route 66 originally crossed into Missouri on the McKinley Bridge in St. Louis, and then in 1929, traffic was shifted to the Municipal Bridge (renamed the MacArthur Bridge in 1942 in honor of General Douglas MacArthur). The roadway on the upper deck was closed in 1981, and Route 66 was later routed over the Mississippi on the north side of St. Louis via the Chain of Rocks Bridge (now closed to vehicular traffic and used as a walking bridge). The remains of the legendary asphalt ribbon still lead us to find the bones of sun-faded signs, buildings long abandoned and choked by vines or trees and the occasional otherworldly occurrence that beckons us out of our warm, safe homes to venture on a journey of the unknown, the "what if" and the wide-eyed hope that something wonderful and chilling lies just beyond our front doors.

BIBLIOGRAPHY

Addams, Jane. "The Devil-Baby at Hull-House." *Atlantic Monthly* 118, no. 4 (October 1916).

———. "A Modern Devil-Baby." *American Journal of Sociology* 20, no. 1 (July 1914).

———. *Women's Memories: Transmuting the Past, as Illustrated by the Story of the Devil Baby*. New York: MacMillan, 1916.

"The Awakening." *A Haunting*. Season 4, episode 2. August 17, 2007.

Babwin, Don. "Forgotten in Death: Cemetery Holds Those Who Died in Prison." *Chicago Tribune*, August 24, 1997.

Bielski, Ursula. *Chicago Haunts: Ghostlore of the Windy City*. Holt, MI: Thunder Bay Press, 2009.

———. *Chicago Haunts 3*. Holt, MI: Thunder Bay Press, 2009.

———. *Creepy Chicago: A Ghosthunter's Tales of the City's Scariest Sites*. Holt, MI: Thunder Bay Press, 2010.

———. *More Chicago Haunts: Scenes from Myth and Memory*. Holt, MI: Thunder Bay Press, 2008.

Booth, Christopher Saint, and Philip Adrian Booth. *The Possessed*. DVD. Spooked TV.

Bosansinga, Jay. "The Sinking of the *Eastland*: America's Forgotten Tragedy." *Chicago Tribune*, June 28, 2005.

Brizzolara, John. "Ghost Hunters: Tales of the Paranormal Steak House." *Chicago Reader*, May 23, 1991.

Chicago Tribune. "Modern Bluebeard: H.H. Holmes' Castle Reveals His True Character." August 18, 1895.

————. "Spotlight: Midlothian—A Spooky Undertaking." October 24, 2006.

Christensen, Jo-Anne. *Ghost Stories of Illinois*. Auburn, WA: Lone Pine Publishing, 2000.

Diskin, Brian, and Gayle Soucek. "Chicago Calamities: Disaster in the Windy City." *Chicago Tribune*, November 29, 2010.

Facchini, Rocco A., and Daniel J. Facchini. *Muldoon, a True Chicago Ghost Story: Tales of a Forgotten Rectory*. Holt, MI: Thunder Bay Press, 2003.

Hauck, Dennis William. *Haunted Places: The National Directory: Ghostly Abodes, Sacred Sites, UFO Landings and Other Supernatural Locations*. New York: Penguin Books, revised edition 2002.

Haunted History: Chicago. DVD. A&E Home Video, 2009.

Hilton, George. "*Eastland*: Legacy of the *Titanic*." *Chicago Tribune*, March 1, 1997.

Hodges, Glenn. "Cahokia: America's Forgotten City." *National Geographic*, January 2011.

Jean-Baptiste, Chantal. "The Excalibur Nightclub and Chicago's First Recorded Murder." Examiner.com. July 10, 2010.

Kachuba, John B. *Ghost Hunting Illinois: America's Haunted Road Trip*. N.p.: Clerisy Press, 2005.

Kay, Margie. *Gateway to the Dead: A Ghost Hunter's Field Guide*. Independence, MO: Nocturna Press, 2013.

Kleen, Michael. *Haunting Illinois: A Tourist's Guide to the Weird and Wild Places of the Prairie State*. Rockford, IL: Black Oak Media, Inc., 2011.

Krist, Gary. "City of Scoundrels: The 12 Days of Disaster That Gave Birth to Modern Chicago." *Chicago Tribune*, April 16, 2013.

Lincoln's New Salem State Park brochure. State of Illinois.

Martin, John Bartlow. "The Master of the Murder Castle: A Classic of Chicago Crime." *Harper's Magazine*, December 1943.

"Midwest Hauntings." *My Ghost Story*. Episode 38.

Moffett, Garret. *Haunted Springfield, Illinois*. Charleston, SC: The History Press, 2011.

Mutual UFO Network (MUFON). http://www.mufon.com.

O'Brien, John. "With One Ruthless Stroke, Al Capone Assumes Undisputed Leadership of Chicago Crime." *Chicago Tribune*, February 13, 1929.

Reader's Digest. *America's Fascinating Indian Heritage—The First Americans: Their Customs, Art, History and How They Lived*. Pleasantville, NY: Reader's Digest Association, 1978.

————. *Quest for the Unknown: Unsolved Mysteries of the Past*. Pleasantville, NY: Reader's Digest Association, A Dorling Kindersley Book, 1991.

Robson, Ellen, and Dianne Halicki. *Haunted Highway: The Spirits of Route 66.* Phoenix, AZ: Golden West Publishers, 1999.

Schechter, Harold. *Depraved: The Definitive True Story of H.H. Holmes, Whose Grotesque Crimes Shattered Turn-of-the-Century Chicago.* New York: Gallery Books, 2008.

Scott, Beth, and Michael Norman. *Haunted Heartland.* New York: Warner Books, 1986.

Snyder, Tom. *Route 66 Traveler's Guide and Roadside Companion.* Collector's edition. New York: St. Martin's Press, 2006.

Southall, Richard. *Haunted Route 66: Ghosts of America's Legendary Highway.* N.p.: Llewellyn Worldwide, 2013.

Stebner, Eleanor. *The Women of Hull House: A Study in Spirituality, Vocation, and Friendship.* Albany: State University of New York Press, 1997

Stevens, E. Winchester. *The Watseka Wonder.* Los Angeles: Austin Publishing Company, 1928.

Suddath, Claire. "Top 10 Evil Liars: Home Is Where the Hate Is." *Time,* May 4, 2011.

Taylor, Troy. *Haunted Illinois: Ghosts and Strange Phenomena of the Prairie State.* N.p.: Stackpole Books, 2008.

———. *The Possessed.* N.p.: Whitechapel Press, 2007.

———. *Weird Chicago.* N.p.: Whitechapel Press, 2008.

Tremeear, Janice. *Missouri's Haunted Route 66: Ghosts Along the Mother Road.* Charleston, SC: The History Press, 2010.

Wachholz, Ted, the Chicago Historical Society and the Eastland Disaster Historical Society. *Images of America: The Eastland Disaster.* Charleston, SC: Arcadia Publishing, 2005.

Young, David. "A Summer Excursion Turns into the Worst Accident in the Annals of Great Lakes Shipping." *Chicago Tribune,* July 24, 1915.

ABOUT THE AUTHOR

Photo by Christina Maharet Hughes for Visions by Maharet.

Janice is a licensed massage therapist (LMT) and energy worker with a third-degree master's certification in Reiki. She is a first order member of the Reformed Druids of Gaia and a member of Mutual UFO Network (MUFON), as well as a staff writer for *Paranormal Investigator Magazine* and contributor to the blogs Sagewoman@Pagasquare and Haunt Jaunts. Drawn into the paranormal as a child, she founded ParaNatural Research Association and spends her time writing about and investigating the paranormal encompassing UFOs, ghosts, aliens, ultraterrestrials and shadow people, experiencing many encounters firsthand.

A featured speaker at the DeSoto Missouri Paracon, VisionCon, St. Louis Pagan Picnic, Ozarks Paracon and the Second-Annual Mid-Continent Paranormal Conference, she's also appeared on radio and TV, particularly *The Itchy Show* (an independent TV program), and participated in an energy experiment with Joshua Shapiro and the Crystal Skull Explorers in October 2011 beginning in Missouri and ending atop Monks Mound at the Cahokia Mounds Historic Site. She contributes to the YouTube program "Silly String Theory," and she and her team will appear in the paranormal/horror movie *Malevolent Entity* for Zomular Media Group LLC. She has four previous books with The History Press.